Taking Measure

Explorations in Number, Architecture and Consciousness

Scott Onstott

Table of Contents

Acknowledgements...i

Introduction..iii

Chapter 1 - The Decimal System and the Ennead 1

Chapter 2 - Metrology...11

Chapter 3 - Measuring Time 41

Chapter 4 - The Honeycomb and the Apple 63

Chapter 5 - Key Numbers 75

Chapter 6 - Number Patterns...99

Chapter 7 - Taxonomy of Encoded Structures..............................121

Chapter 8 - Encoded Structures 135

Chapter 9 - Behind the Curtain 149

About the Author 166

Acknowledgements

I am blessed to have daily contact with fans from all over the world. A warm thank you to all those who email me, post thoughtful comments on my blog, and/or interact with me on Facebook.

I am especially grateful to my wife Jenn Nelson and my friend Ian le Cheminant for their insightful editing of this book.

Introduction

I began this book as a way of taking measure of my two films, Secrets In Plain Sight Volumes 1 & 2, a series very densely packed with information which runs for more than 5 hours. Many viewers watch the films over and over and have picked up different things on each viewing. This process takes a lot of time and I recognize that people are very busy these days so I wanted to distill into a small book the essentials of what the films have uncovered. The written format encourages depth of analysis and synthesis.

By taking measure of the objective world of things from the quantum to architectural to astronomic scales, I have observed numerical patterns emerging from the scientific data. This book presents numeric codes unfolding in space and time in many unexpected places, from our units of measure to the relationships between celestial bodies. Geometric and numeric encoding is also explored in cities, in architecture, in alignments across the Earth, and in the human body. We start in the exterior objective world and the evidence gradually leads us into the subjective world within.

As I set off writing I didn't realize the extent to which this book would clarify my own thinking and take my awareness in new directions but that was the end result. I hope that by reading this book you will enjoy the journey and the expanded perspectives as much as I do.

Scott Onstott
Cortes Island, British Columbia, Canada
November 2012

Chapter 1 - The Decimal System and the Ennead

The decimal system is used throughout the world today. As children we learned that the string of digits 1111 means one thousand plus one hundred plus ten plus one. The place a digit occupies in a number encodes its order of magnitude.

The numeral base is so much a part of our subconscious minds that few people are aware that the decimal system is known formally as base ten, let alone take the time to ponder the possibility of using other numeral bases.

The Mayans used base twenty (called vigesimal) and the Babylonians used base sixty (called sexagesimal) that we still employ to measure time.

You probably already know that computers process nothing but ones and zeros. Using only 1 and 0 is known as base two. Binary digits double in value in each place; the first place represents 1, the second place represents 2, the third place represents 4, the fourth place represents 8, and so on. The binary number 1111 therefore encodes 8+4+2+1 or the decimal number 15. The transistor, which is really just a very tiny electronic door, can either be open or closed, 1 or 0. Base two is therefore the most efficient choice to represent binary electronic states.

Web designers know that color is efficiently expressed using hexadecimal codes, which are base 16. In hexadecimal, letters A-F are used in addition to the Arabic numerals 1-9 in order to complete the full complement of the fifteen required digits plus zero.

The base is always one unit higher than the number of possible digits used, precisely because of the magic of zero. Nothingness is a strange magic because strictly speaking zero doesn't really exist even though for practical purposes it is commonly considered to be a digit. How can nothing be something? Zero is simply a place holder, an emptiness. In base ten the number 10 encodes one ten and no ones. We need the zero so that 1 can be recognized as being in the second place. The place assigns the digit 1 the quantity of ten. Without the invention of zero we would be hard-pressed to calculate anything. What is DCLXVI times DLV in Roman numerals?

Zero was a great invention and base ten is just an arbitrary convention allowing us to get on with buying and selling, so what of it?

This chapter aims to show why the choice of base ten is anything but arbitrary because the decimal system literally underlies the structure of physical reality.

Many people assume we use base ten because we have ten digits on our hands (counting fingers and thumbs as equal digits). However this assumption is flawed. Follow the assumption to its logical conclusion: with ten digits we should be using base eleven. Remember the base has to be one numeral higher than the full complement of digits because we must also account for the placeholder zero.

Which one of your fingers is your zeroth digit? Kids don't start counting fingers with zero and if you do start counting with 1 you shouldn't end with 10 either because 10 presupposes the complex concept of place and the void (0) to hold the ones place open. If you were designing a numeral system based on your hands then you wouldn't stop on your last little finger and have to go into abstract philosophical explanations with an appeal to nothingness to name it. You might symbolize it with an X like the Romans did and be done with it. The concept of zero didn't occur to the Romans (we have 9th century India to thank for zero).

However, ever since Fibonacci, we in the West are quite familiar with the magic of zero and therefore when we count our fingers we call our last little finger number 10 without thinking much of it. However, if the decimal system isn't based on our hands then what is its basis?

To answer this fundamental question I turn to the research of Dr. Peter Plichta, who holds a PhD in physics and another in chemistry. In his book God's Secret Formula: Deciphering the Riddle of the Universe and the Prime Number Code (Element 1997) he realized the significance of there being exactly 81 stable atoms in the universe.

The periodic table of the elements shows atomic numbers higher than 83 as subject to radioactive decay. In addition, elements 43 (Technetium) and 61 (Promethium) also radioactively decay. In time all radioactive elements naturally split into one or more of the stable elements. Plichta asked himself, "Why should precisely 81 stable elements exist, no more, and no less?"

Plichta found the answer in the reciprocal of 81. He discovered the following relationship:

$1/81 = .0123456789(10)(11)(12)(13)...$

The reciprocal of 81 is a sequence of all whole numbers after the decimal point. Whole numbers higher than 9 are shown in parentheses because no numeral higher than 9 can exist in the decimal place system. Converting this infinite string of numbers into the decimal system yields the infinitely recurring number:

0.01234567912345679...

In other words the digit 8 is always missing from the pattern. To convince yourself of the veracity of this fact consider that $1/81 = 1/9 \times 1/9$. One ninth equals 0.111111... Multiplying a string of ones times a string of ones yields a sub-total of one in every place. Adding up columns of sequentially increasing ones logically results in a string of numbers from the void all the way to infinity. When these numbers are put into the decimal system, the numbers higher than 9 are carried into adjacent places, and the digit 8 somewhat mysteriously disappears from the answer.

A similar symmetry can be seen in the fact that $12345679 \times 9 = 111,111,111$.

You can also think of 81 as a poetic metaphor for "infinite one"; what is the numeral 8 but the infinity symbol turned on its side?

In ancient Heliopolis (today a district of modern Cairo) the Egyptians venerated a pantheon of 9 gods that the Greeks called the ennead, meaning a collection of nine things. I think the ennead, among many other layers of meaning, was intended to be an analogy for the decimal system. For more than two thousand years until the first millennium BC the Egyptians used hieroglyphic numerals that were based on a decimal system.

Could it be that the ancient Egyptian gods themselves ultimately represented numbers? The Greek philosopher Pythagoras, who was educated in Heliopolis, Egypt, is known for saying "All is number."

Atum was considered to be the first god and creator of the universe. The other deities and all physical things were said to be "made of Atum's flesh" according to Richard Wilkinson in The Complete Gods and Goddesses of Ancient Egypt (2003). The total number of one-to-one interactions amongst the ennead (order being significant) yields 81 possible relationships as 9 times 9 is 81. I see the ennead's web of interaction precisely expressing the number of stable atoms in our universe. It makes perfect sense that we are all made of Atum's flesh because atoms are what the physical universe is made of.

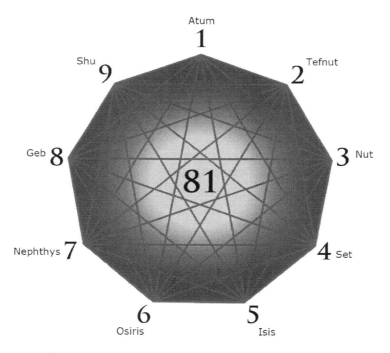

I have assigned the number 1 to the creator Atum. He created Shu and Tefnut first. They mated and Tefnut gave birth to Geb and Nut. They in turn mated and Nut gave birth to the remaining gods. So my strategy was to assign the gods from the top down equally on both sides of the diagram. One can debate whether Shu should be 2 and Tefnut 9 for example, and so on. Isis as goddess of nature seems to resonate with 5, the number of life. Osiris as Lord of the Dead resonates with the number of lifeless structure or 6. I go into the qualities of 6 and 5 in Chapter 4 - The Honeycomb and the Apple.

If the universe is a matrix of the numbers 1, 2, 3, 4, 5, 6, 7, 8 and 9 whose interactions in some unseen way continually manifest all the atoms in the void (with 0 representing empty space) then it is certainly fortuitous that we are so familiar with the decimal system because physical reality appears to be fundamentally structured on base ten.

I discovered a nine-sided polygon encoded in San Francisco resonating with the ennead.

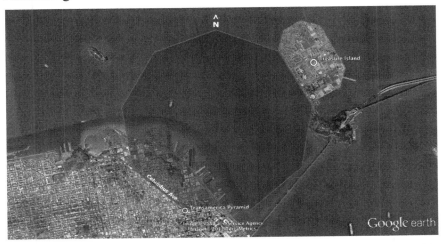

The Transamerica Pyramid is at the vertex corresponding with Osiris in the ennead. Moving clockwise, Columbus Avenue runs along the edge that begins at the Pyramid, the oldest street grid of the city runs parallel to the next edge, the top vertex of the enneagon points due north, and Treasure Island's location, orientation, and edge length matches the corresponding edge of the diagram. The natural Yerba Buena Island fronts the adjacent edge.

Treasure Island is an artificial island that is part of the city and county of San Francisco. Construction started in 1936 in preparation for the Golden Gate International Exposition.

Much of my research presented in Secrets in Plain Sight - Volumes 1 & 2 (and in my blog) consistently leads back to ancient Egypt. However I do not think that the ancient Egyptians are the ultimate source of the wisdom. Perhaps one reason why ancient Egyptian symbolism is so often used in modern structures is because Egypt's desert climate has preserved many artifacts and temples so we know a great deal about this particular ancient culture.

Many other ancient cultures hold tantalizing clues to the Great Mystery such as the Sumerian, the Vedic culture in India, the Toltec culture in the Americas, the Chinese, the megalithic building cultures of old Europe, and many others. The most ancient temples all around the world seem to encode the greatest wisdom and subsequent eras show degradation of construction techniques and encoded knowledge until the understanding appears to have gone underground during the dark ages in Europe. The wisdom resurfaced with the flowering of the Gothic style in the 12th century and has been kept alive up to the present day in secret societies such as the Templars and Masonic orders.

Number Quality

We are accustomed to thinking of numbers as quantities. How many widgets? How much money? However, in addition to representing quantities, numbers also have qualities in themselves.

The quality of the number 1 is unity. We are all ultimately one. We are all Atum's flesh if you will. We all are parts of one giant mind. This is the profound spiritual truth expressed in many of the world's religions and in recent experiments in consciousness (see www.1giantmind.org/?page_id=216).

The quality of the number 2 is duality. Good/evil, day/night, hot/cold, male/female, and so on are mirrored in the left/right hemispheres of the brain and the bilateral symmetry of our bodies. Each one of the numbers 1, 2, 3, 4, 5, 6, 7, 8, and 9 have specific characters. I think the Egyptians expressed this in their mythologies about Atum, Shu, Tefnut, Geb, Nut, Set, Isis, Osiris, and Nephthys (the ennead).

There is a lot to say about number quality and I recommend reading Michael Schneider's book The Beginner's Guide to Constructing the Universe: The Mathematical Archetypes of Nature, Art, and Science (Harper Perennial 1995) for an excellent introduction.

The final level of number quality is multiplicity. In other words these are the combinations of numbers flowing out from the ennead, namely all integers 10 and higher. Within the multiplicity I see many specific numbers that express essential qualities, such as the numbers 24, 33, 36, 153, 273, 400, 528, 720 and many more.

Repetitive Single Digits

Repetitive single digits are commonly encountered in distances, headings with respect to true north, in architecture, in building addresses, dates, and even in the time of day. A few examples of numbers with repetitive single digits are the Masonic Center at 1111 California Street in San Francisco, the 33.33 degree distance from Stonehenge to the Dome of the Rock in Jerusalem, the 555'5.5" height of the Washington Monument, the 66.66 nautical miles from Silbury Hill (tallest prehistoric human-made mound in Europe) to the Shard (tallest building in the EU), the 4444 day gap between the start date of the first Gulf War and the second Gulf War, and how Remembrance day is celebrated at the 11th hour of the 11th day of the 11th month annually.

I will explain why finding patterns in various units of measure is an acceptable practice in the next chapter on Metrology.

There are of course nine possible repetitive single digits in the decimal system (1-9) and no matter how many zeros are repeated the value and meaning of any string of zeros is zero. Repetitive single digits 1 through 9 emphasize number quality, that is the character of the individual numbers of the ennead.

Take for example the Washington Monument's height of 555'5.5." The repetition of fives should draw our attention to the essential quality of 5. The monument's height resonates with fiveness, which I correlate with Isis in the ennead.

It just so happens that 555'5.5" equals 6666" if you round up to the nearest inch.

Therefore the monument also resonates with 6 which I correlate with Osiris. The monument is really an expression of the relationship between Osiris and Isis or 6 to 5. The chapter entitled The Honeycomb and the Apple delves into the fundamental relationship of 6 to 5.

The word rational comes from making a ratio between two numbers. Rationally speaking, the essential and eternal quality of each number 1 through 9 is revealed when it is compared to the whole of the ennead. In other words, all ninths produce eternally repeating single digits.

$1/9 = .111111...$
$2/9 = .222222...$
$3/9 = .333333... = 1/3$
$4/9 = .444444...$
$5/9 = .555555...$
$6/9 = .666666... = 2/3$
$7/9 = .777777...$
$8/9 = .888888...$
$9/9 = .999999... = 1$

Digital Roots

The concept of reducing any multi-digit number down to a single digit goes by many names such as Pythagorean addition, Theosophical addition, Kabbalistic addition, reduced ordinal values, horizontal addition, modulo 9 arithmetic, number essence, decimal parity, or digital root. I'll use the term digital root to refer to this practice.

For example, the number 12 can be reduced to a digital root of 3 because $1+2 = 3$. You will always be left with exactly one numeral for any digital root, be it 1 2, 3, 4, 5, 6, 7, 8, or 9. The digital root of zero is zero.

Larger numbers sometimes require intermediate subtotals to arrive at a singular digital root. The number 25,920's digital root is 9 because $2+5+9+2+0 = 18$ and $1+8 = 9$.

'Digital Roots' by Scott Onstott

The practice of finding digital roots is an attempt to distill quality from quantity.

Chapter 2 - Metrology

Metrology is the science of measurement. If you assume that measurement sounds uninteresting I hope this chapter changes your mind.

Measuring allows us to quantify the universe. Harmonic units of measure reveal patterns, key numbers, and fundamental relationships that have the potential to alter one's awareness of reality.

Alexander Thom was a Scottish engineer who from 1933 to 1977 surveyed 600 sites from the Neolithic period in the UK and France and deduced a unit of measure used in their construction. Thom named this unit the megalithic yard. Designers tend to lay out structures in whole numbers no matter what units they are using.

For example, the dimensions of Solomon's temple are given in the Bible as 60 cubits long, 20 cubits wide, and 30 cubits high. The practicality of using integer dimensions makes it possible to reverse engineer the unit of measure from built structures.

I have noticed that many units of measure commonly used today harmonize with the size, rate of rotation, period of revolution, and precessional cycle of the Earth. Specific units of measure reveal key numbers, which resonate with many of the metrological parameters of Earth, Moon, and Sun.

In ancient Egypt, metrology was closely associated with the goddess Seshet, goddess of architecture, astronomy, mathematics, measurement, and surveying. She was also known as Mistress of the House of Scrolls, having been credited with the invention of writing. Her priests in Heliopolis oversaw the library where the most important knowledge and wisdom was preserved (but unfortunately lost thousands of years ago).

Later in Egyptian history when the god Thoth became prominent, Seshet's role changed and she became his wife or daughter. The word "sesheta" means hidden things, mysteries, or secrets. So the implication is that the initiate was being given access to secret mysteries through the goddess Seshet.

The Pyramid Texts are composed of what Egyptologists call "spells" or "utterances" carved on walls and sarcophagi of pharaohs during the Old Kingdom and are the oldest known religious texts in the world. In contrast to these earliest texts, ordinary Egyptians who could afford a coffin wrote the Coffin Texts just after the Old Kingdom. Spell 10 of the Coffin Texts states "Seshat opens the door of heaven for you." Metrology is truly one of the keys to the mysteries.

Shifting Decimal Places

The following metrological statements all have the same number quality:

The Sun's diameter is 864,000 miles (99.9%).

There are exactly 86,400 seconds in a mean solar day.

The distance between Stonehenge and Silbury Hill is 86,400 feet.*

Silbury Hill was designed using integer multiples of an 8.64 foot unit.*

The implied rectangle encompassing London's Olympic Stadium is 80,640 square meters (315m x 256m).**

The Parliamentary Triangle in Canberra Australia has a perimeter of 8640 meters.**

One day and night of Brahma in Hindu time reckoning is 8,640,000,000 years.

* Discovered by John Michell and Robin Heath in The Lost Science of Measuring the Earth (Adventures Unlimited Press 2006)

** Discovered by Jan Thulstrup

Each of the above facts expresses the character of the number 864. It doesn't matter how many zeros are inserted amongst the digits because they hold places indicating quantity rather than quality. You can think of shifting decimal places as equivalent to scaling up or scaling down by arbitrary orders of magnitude. The transformation of scale does not change any quality of the numbers nor does it change the esoteric meaning.

Understanding Accuracy

For values in this book which are not exact, I often give accuracy values as percentages in parentheses such as the Sun's diameter is 864,000 miles (99.9%).

If you look up Sun on Wikipedia you will find that its mean diameter is 1,392,684 kilometers which equals 865,373.7 miles.

Some might see the actual solar diameter in miles and think my statement is not good enough. The Sun is over one thousand miles larger in diameter than the quoted 864,000 miles. In our earthly experience a thousand miles is a long way.

864,000 miles has three significant figures. To make a valid determination of accuracy we must compare the numbers at the same level of precision. Dividing 864,000 by 865,000 yields 0.999 which is 99.9%. A thousand miles turns out to be a trivial distance in the diameter of our incredibly large Sun. We are tolerating a tiny error in order to perceive the larger pattern that resonates with the key number 864.

If I claim my car is blue and a skeptic says no it is not, but in actual fact the car is 99.9% blue and 0.1% red you would immediately see the absurdity of the skeptic not perceiving the overwhelming reality. After all, nothing in physical reality is exactly perfect. Debating tenths of one percent inaccuracy in a correlation is to miss the point.

There will always be a slight gap between the real and the ideal. A geometric example of this gap is the difference between the Fibonacci spiral and the golden spiral.

The Fibonacci spiral is built with squares having edge lengths of 1,1,2,3,5,8,13,34,55, and so on. Each term in the Fibonacci sequence is the sum of the preceding two terms. Sunflowers exhibit Fibonacci spiral patterning in the positioning of their seeds which are necessarily formed in discrete units. The Fibonacci spiral is shown in the upper part of the diagram.

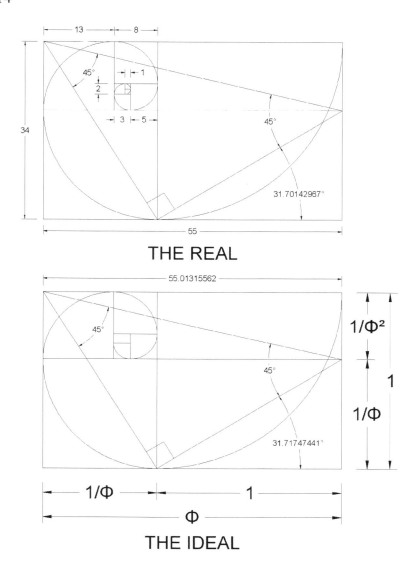

THE REAL

THE IDEAL

The golden spiral is based on the irrational number 1.618099389... which is called Phi after the Greek letter. The golden spiral is shown in the lower diagram and its exact Phi proportions are shown in a larger font.

Phi is an important and fundamental structure of reality. The real version is ever so slightly off compared to the ideal version. The ~32 degree angle in the real version is 99.9% accurate when compared to the ideal version.

Another example of the discrepancy between the real and the ideal is the concept of the Pythagorean Comma in musical tuning. The perfect fifth is universally perceived as the most harmonious musical interval aside from the octave itself. If you play a series of notes ascending in a series of 12 justly tuned perfect fifths you will come extremely close to a note, which is exactly 7 octaves above the original note (99%). The difference is slight but perceptible. The Comma has vexed musicians and philosophers for centuries because it reveals the irreconcilable and ever-present difference between the real and the ideal.

Understanding Precision

Significant digits carry meaning describing the precision of real world measurements. For example 33.33 is one hundred times more precise than 33 because it has two more significant decimal places.

The number 33, having two significant digits, might actually measure anywhere from 32.5 to 33.5 and still be rounded to 33. It is optional to round up or down when 5 is the place value to be rounded off (32.5 could be rounded to 32 or 33 but 32.6 should be rounded to 33).

The Dome of the Rock in Jerusalem is 33 miles from the sea, a fact that is precise to two significant digits. The Dome of the Rock is 33.33 degrees from Stonehenge. We don't normally measure distances in degrees but this is possible in Google Earth, which compensates for the variable length of degrees across Earth's surface (more on Google Earth and degrees later in this chapter).

The statement that the Sun's diameter is 864,000 miles has three significant digits and an accuracy of (99.9%).

Light takes 3.3 nanoseconds to travel one meter. This statement is precise to two significant digits.

Calculations performed on significant digits cannot be done with greater precision than the original data. Taking the reciprocal of the speed of light (1 / 299,792,458 meters per second) equals 3.3 nanoseconds per meter. This massive reduction in significant figures is acceptable because it is a true statement albeit less precise.

However you can't start with a measurement of 3.3 nanoseconds per meter and with its reciprocal, produce a value more precise than two significant figures. Given initial data of 3.3 nanoseconds per meter, you could take its reciprocal and produce a value of 300 million meters per second—in this case the first two digits of 300 million are significant. There are rules determining whether to treat digits as significant that you can easily Google.

There is a difference between precision and exactness. The answer to the mathematical statement 332 + 1 is 333 exactly. This is true to an infinite number of decimal places because 333 is an exact quantity in this context, rather than a measurement.

You can count exactly 333 apples but in any measurement significant figures are implied, such as the 333 foot height of the George Washington Masonic National Memorial. This replica of the Lighthouse of Alexandria Egypt, wonder of the ancient world, was completed in 1932 in Alexandria Virginia.

Pi is the relationship between a circle's circumference and its diameter. Pi is a transcendental number having an infinite number of significant digits. 22/7 and 864/275 are rational approximations of Pi which also have infinite numbers of significant digits. No matter how precise the approximations are, they are not as accurate in describing the circumference/diameter relationship as Pi is.

Accuracy is more important than precision but you can't have accuracy without sufficient precision. Precision improves with the number of significant figures. However, you can have an infinite number of significant figures but still not be accurate. When a value has high precision and accuracy then you are assured of having a quality measurement.

Measuring with Google Earth

Taking measurements with Google Earth is straightforward. I will walk you through one such measurement in case you've never done this sort of thing before. Don't take my word for anything you doubt. Check things out for yourself in Google Earth, or look up facts on Google, Wikipedia, in books, or using alternative methods.

You can download Google Earth from http://earth.google.com for Windows and Mac OS. The iPad / iPhone Google Earth apps unfortunately don't have measurement functionality as of the date of this book's publication and, to the best of my knowledge you won't be able to measure using Google Earth in other ebook readers.

You don't need the Google Earth Pro version for this - the Google Earth free version is just as accurate. I'm using the Pro version and you'll see a few extra buttons in the Ruler dialog box but don't let that distract you.

Click the Show Ruler button on the toolbar and a floating Ruler dialog box will appear. Zoom into the area you want to start measuring from. Roll the mouse wheel to zoom in and out and drag the mouse to move over the Earth. For example, type Jerusalem in the search box and press Enter to fly there. Locate the Dome of the Rock on the Temple Mount. For this you can turn on the Wikipedia or Photos layers if you are unfamiliar with the old city's appearance from space. When you have located the octagonal Dome of the Rock with its gold roof, click right in the center of the building, as best as you can visually estimate.

Now type Stonehenge in the search box and press Enter to fly there. Zoom in until you can clearly see the ancient structure. Click the center of Stonehenge to locate the endpoint of your line that now stretches all the way from the Dome of the Rock.

Open the flyout menu that displays units of measure in the Ruler dialog box. Select Degrees and you will now see that Stonehenge really is 33.33 degrees from the Dome of the Rock.

Click the Save button in the Ruler dialog box. To give the path a name, type *Dome of the Rock to Stonehenge* and click OK. This path appears under Places for future reference.

Zoom way out until you can see the whole path. Drag the mouse wheel to tilt your perspective so you can see the curvature of the Earth. The straight-line path you have just drawn is actually the shortest distance between the Dome of the Rock and Jerusalem. It follows the curvature of the Earth so it appears curved from oblique angles and straight when viewed directly above.

Lines in Google Earth are approximated by portions of great circles whose centers coincide with the center of the Earth. The Earth is not a true sphere but rather has a complex curvature called the geoid (the Earth is slightly compressed at the poles as compared to the equator but there are also more subtle local variations in curvature).

The heading value in the Ruler dialog box is the bearing of the line toward its endpoint measured clockwise from true north in degrees.

The heading between the Dome of the Rock and Stonehenge is 317 degrees.

The heading between Stonehenge and the Dome of the Rock is 111 degrees.

Headings are different at each endpoint of the path. Notice also that 317 minus 180 does not equal 111 (it is 137). In other words the headings at either end are not facing back in the opposite direction. This is because headings are not constant along the shortest path between two points on the globe (unless you are headed in the cardinal directions).

If you journey with a constant heading you will actually traverse a curving path called a rhumb line. All rhumb lines eventually end up at either the North Pole or the South Pole. Google Earth cannot measure or plot rhumb lines. Pilots and mariners traditionally travel rhumb lines from waypoint to waypoint. At each convenient waypoint they adjust their heading to approximate the shortest straight-line path to their destination which continually changes bearings.

John Michell and Christine Rhone described a rhumb line in Twelve Tribe Nations: Sacred Number and the Golden Age (Inner Traditions 2008). Their Apollo-Michael rhumb line connects numerous shrines dedicated to the pagan Sun God and Christian Archangel. I created this visualization of the Apollo-Michael rhumb line outside of Google Earth.

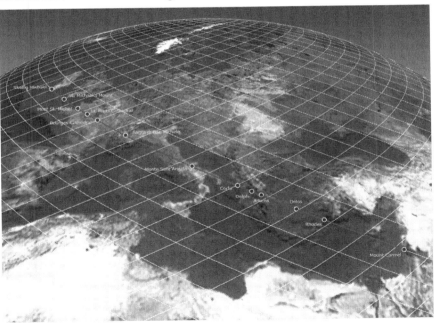

Google Earth is an incredible tool that literally puts the whole virtual world at your fingertips. By exploring accurate digital models of the Earth a growing number of researchers are beginning to discover a structure to reality that few in our time have perceived.

Measuring Geographic Coordinates and Angles

The Babylonians were the first culture that we know of to divide the circle into 360 degrees, based on their sexagesimal (base 60) number system. Perhaps we still consider 360 degrees a full circle today because 360 has so many factors: 1, 2, 3, 4, 5, 6, 8, 9, 10, 12, 15, 18, 20, 24, 30, 36, 40, 45, 60, 72, 90, 120, 180, and 360. This large quantity of factors makes it easy to measure angles using integers for most practical tasks.

We use sexagesimal notation in measuring geographic coordinates, angles, and time. We divide 360 degrees each into 60 minute parts, called *minutes* (all that is required is a shift of accent on the word). For even more precision we divide minutes a second time into another 60 parts, and we appropriately call these *seconds*.

It is amazing to me that Babylonians, founders of the sexagesimal system that is used to map the world, located their capital city at 32 deg 32 min 32 sec N latitude. Were they aware of the amazing resonance of the key number 32 or is this simply a coincidence?

This scheme of division into minutes and seconds allows us to be precise when dividing a full circle into any number of parts, even when the parts aren't factors of 360. For example, consider dividing a circle into 7 parts. What angle does one of these parts have? 360 / 7 = 51.4286 degrees. The decimal form is harder to use from a practical standpoint than the sexagesimal form when it comes to locating geographic coordinates on the ground.

For example, another way of looking at a 7th part division of the circle is as 51 degrees 25 minutes 43 seconds. This is the exact northern latitude of Avebury, a famous Neolithic henge in the UK.

A series of ancient temples were located by dividing a quadrant of the Earth (from the equator to the pole) into 7 parts.

1. Aden, Yemen: 90 x (1/7) = 12 deg, 51 min, 26 sec N (exact)
2. Temple of Karnak, Egypt: 90 x (2/7) = 25 deg, 42 min, 51 sec N (exact)
3. Delphi, Greece: 90 x (3/7) = 38 deg, 34 min, 17 sec N (off by 5 min)
4. Avebury, UK: 90 x (4/7) = 51 deg, 25 min, 43 sec N (exact)
5. Thingvellir, Iceland: 90 x (6/7) = 77 deg, 8 min, 34 sec N (off by 1 min)

The French made several attempts to institute decimal time starting in 1793 but it never caught on having 10 decimal hours a day, 100 decimal minutes, and 100 decimal seconds. What time was that again?

We are much more comfortable with Hours:Minutes based notation such as 10:08 AM meaning 10 hours and 8 minutes after midnight. It is amazing that this particular time is used in the majority of clock and watch advertisements worldwide. Consider also that the combined diameters of Earth and Moon are 10,080 miles (99.96%).

See Secrets In Plain Sight - Volume 2 for more information on the 10:08 phenomenon and how it encodes the slope of the Great Pyramid as well as encoding the position of the Louvre pyramid based on the azimuth of summer solstice sunrise. My discoveries in this regard build on the work of Bert Janssen who originally connected the time 10:08 to squaring the circle and also to the Mayan calendar.

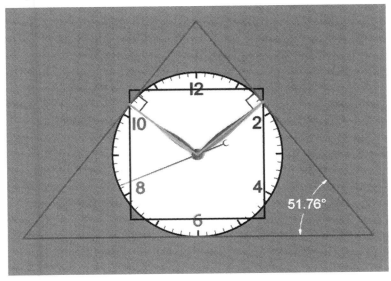

Hugh Newman noted in <u>Earth Grids: The Secret Patterns of Gaia's Sacred Sites</u> (Wooden Books 2008) that the Kaaba in Mecca is at the golden latitude, a parallel that divides the distance from pole to pole by Phi (180 / 1.62 = 111.111... degrees).

The Eastern cornerstone of the Kaaba contains fragments of the Black Stone, venerated at the site long before Muhammad was born. Muslim tradition holds that the black stone fell from heaven to show Adam and Eve where to build an altar. In fact the Kaaba is 11.1 miles north of the exact golden latitude.

It is interesting that the Kaaba itself is a black cube. There is a resonance between the symbol of the black cube and Saturn. A cube viewed at an angle appears as a hexagon. As it happens there is a persisting hexagonal wave pattern around the north pole of Saturn. This large scale structure was discovered by Voyager 1 in 1980 and confirmed by the Cassini spacecraft in 2006.

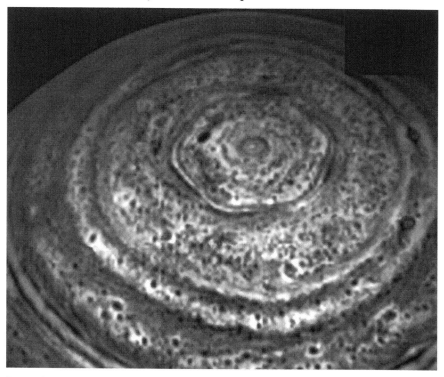

Image from NASA's Cassini spacecraft

It is astounding to see such pure geometry on the scale of a planet. The straight sides of the hexagon are each approximately 8640 miles long (note the solar number) which is longer than the diameter of the Earth.

Saturn takes 29.5 years to revolve around the Sun. Coincidentally the Moon takes 29.5 days to orbit the Earth with respect to the Sun. Saturn the planet and god of time appears to be synchronized with the lunar month and the Earth year.

Every cube has 6 faces. If each face is assigned an edge length of 6 units then the volume and surface areas are harmonized, as they are both given by the equation 6 x 6 x 6 = 216.

Another way of analyzing a cube is to find the sum of its angles. Every angle in a cube is of course a right angle, so 90 degrees per angle x 3 angles at each corner x 8 corners = 2160 degrees. 2160 is also the number of miles in the Moon's diameter (99.9%). This is especially resonant with Islam as the Muslim calendar is lunar and the crescent moon is the symbol used on top of many important Islamic structures.

Immediately adjacent to the Kaaba's Grand Mosque, largest in the world, stands the Mecca Royal Hotel Clock Tower complex. It holds many world records including tallest clock tower, largest clock face, largest floor area, tallest hotel, and second tallest building in the world. The clock tower lifts the crescent moon to the highest heights on Earth.

Image credit Syed Moizuddin and Rohith Manoragan under the Creative Commons Attribution-Sharealike 3.0 license

The black foundation stone in Mecca reminds me of the foundation stone at 111 Cannon Street in the heart of the City of London. This stone laid by the Romans was the origin point of all distances measured in England. These stones are in the tradition of the *Umbilicus Urbis Romae*, and the omphalos stone at Delphi, each marking an axis mundi or the center of a world coordinate system.

The London stone was originally located on the south side of Cannon street. When it became an obstacle to traffic it was relocated across the street to its present location in 1742 AD.

Cleopatra's Needle, an ancient Egyptian obelisk originally from Heliopolis, sits on the Victoria embankment of the Thames, 2160 meters from the original location of the London stone. By the way, the Thames River was originally called *The Isis* and still bears this name in Oxford.

The latitude of the original location of the London stone is 51.5114 deg N. This is amazing because the slope angle of the Great Pyramid is 51 deg 51 min 14 sec, as measured from its few remaining casing stones. This play on numbers between the decimal and degrees-minutes-seconds systems is interesting.

The London stone rests at the base of a street pyramid in the oldest part of Roman Londinium.

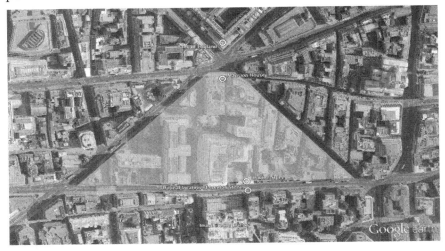

Mansion House at the top of the pyramid is the official residence of the Lord Mayor of London. The main reception room is called the Egyptian Hall because it uses an arrangement of columns deemed to be Egyptian by the Roman architect Vitruvius. It is adjacent to the Mithraeum; a Temple of Mithras was discovered within the street pyramid in 1954.

From Arc Measure to Linear Measure

Ship captains traditionally measured the globe just as we measure angles in geometry - in degrees, minutes, and seconds. This is ideal for plotting one's position on a map. Quantifying how fast one was going and thus, how long it would take to get somewhere was, however, another matter. Mariners originally solved the rate problem with a long coil of knotted rope tied to a log. The log was thrown overboard and left to drift in the water as the ship sailed on. As the rope was drawn out, the number of knots that went overboard was counted while sand passed through a glass measuring a fixed amount of time. The number of knots was entered in a book made of wooden shingles that became known as the ship's log (see http://1.usa.gov/SIA5cU).

The knots in the rope became the *knot*, a unit of speed equal to one sea mile per hour. A sea mile is for any latitude the length of one minute of latitude at that latitude. The knot is a bridge between arc measure and linear measure on the Earth.

An added complexity is that the length of the sea mile varies by about 1% from the equator to the pole, getting longer as one sails to higher latitudes due to Earth's equatorial bulge. To even out this error, the international nautical mile (NM) was defined in 1929 as one mean sea mile in whole meters, which turns out to be 1852 meters.

So 1 NM is the linear measurement equal to 1 mean minute of arc along any meridian.

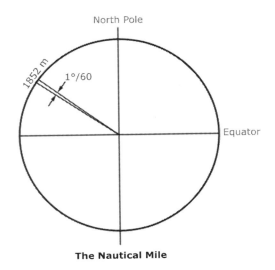

The Nautical Mile

The Earth's meridional circumference is therefore approximated by 360 degrees x 60 minutes = 21,600 nautical miles, or 6 x 6 x 6 x 100 nautical miles.

60 NM = 1 mean degree of arc = 111.1 kilometers.

The *world geodetic system* (WGS) is a standard used for cartography, geodesy, and navigation. It defines an oblate spheroid surface that represents nominal sea level. The system was created in 1984 but last revised in 2004. The latest revision is referred to as WGS84, named after the year of the system's founding. The global positioning system, powered by GPS satellites, uses WGS84 as its reference coordinate system.

In WGS84 at the equator, 1 degree of latitude is equivalent to 111 km, and 1 degree of longitude is equivalent to 111 km.

Do you see the recurring pattern of repetitive single digits encoded into the Earth and our units of measure used to quantify its dimensions? I discuss why this might be so in Chapter 9 - Behind the Curtain but you might want to wait to look behind it until later.

Here are a few significant measurements I've made in nautical miles for your consideration:

The distance from Silbury Hill to the Shard at 32 London Bridge

Street (tallest building in London) is 66.66 NM. There is one structure 66 feet taller in the UK but it's not considered a building: the Emley Moor transmitting station stands 330 meters in height.

The distance from the Great Pyramid in Egypt to Delphi in Greece is 666 NM.

The distance from the Kaaba in Mecca to the Dome of the Rock in Jerusalem is 666 NM.

The distance from the Kaaba in Mecca to the temple of Baalbek in Lebanon is 777 NM.

Imperial Measure

We were taught in school that the English foot was the length of some king's big foot. Some probably wondered whether the foot is therefore as arbitrary as the institution of monarchy.

However, I beg to differ on one point. Giving up your personal power to an "authority" set above you is never a wise idea, but the English foot and the Imperial system of measurement are far older than the English empire, and probably older than the institution of monarchy as well.

I will present four different systems showing how the inch, foot, furlong, mile, and ancient Egyptian cubits are hyper-dimensionally interconnected.

The first system is the obscure *furlong*, which is a distance exactly equal to 660 feet. The furlong is a traditional unit of measure that has mostly been forgotten. However the furlong is still used in horse racing; for example the Kentucky Derby is a 10-furlong race.

The acre was originally defined as a unit of land area measuring one furlong long by one chain (another nearly forgotten unit) wide. It just so happens that my rural property deed in Canada where I reside is measured in chains. One chain equals 66 feet.

1 acre = 1 furlong x 1 chain = 660 feet x 66 feet.

Incidentally 5 furlongs is 3,300 feet which is approximately equal to 1 kilometer (99%).

There are exactly 8 furlongs in a mile.

The above facts might be interesting, but I want to draw your attention to the following correlation:

1 furlong = 660 feet = 7920 inches.
Earth's mean diameter is 7920 miles (99.97%).

In this way the furlong resonates with the Earth through the Imperial system.

*****

Before reaching our eyes, the light from the Sun travels a distance equal to what is called one *astronomical unit*, which is defined as the mean distance from the Sun to the Earth. The astronomical unit is helpful in making comparisons to the orbits of other planets in our solar system.

The universe is so vast, as you know, that astronomers measure even larger distances in terms of *light-years*, the distance light travels in the time it takes the Earth to revolve once around the Sun (our solar year).

Lawrence Edlund discovered that if the astronomical unit is compared to an inch then a light year would be equal to one mile (99.9%). Another way of expressing this is in the following ratios:

1 inch / 1 mile = 1 astronomical unit / 1 light-year

Thus the relationship of the inch to the mile resonates with the distance between the Earth and Sun, the time it takes the Earth to orbit the Sun, and the speed of light.

*****

The next system comes from a discovery published in The Lost Science of Measuring the Earth (Adventures Unlimited Press 2006) by John Michell and Robin Heath. They made the following claim:

Earth's equatorial circumference = 365.242 x 360 x 1000 feet

In other words the number of days in a solar year times the number of degrees in a circle times a scaling value of 1000 equals the Earth's maximum circumference in feet.

The system used by GPS satellites - WGS84 - lists the Earth's equatorial circumference as 24,901.4 miles and if you do the math the accuracy of the above claim is 99.99%. This is an astounding level of accuracy with error down to one hundredth of one percent; it is off by just 1 mile!

Therefore the foot has been non-randomly defined to encode the time it takes the Earth to orbit the Sun, the measurement of a circle in degrees (which is implied in any orbit), and a scaling factor of 3 orders of magnitude.

The last system is a series of discoveries I made revealing profound connections between inches, feet, cubits, miles, the size of the Earth, the Great Pyramid, the location of Memphis, and much else besides.

First we need some background. WGS84 accurately defines the following parameters of the Earth:

Meridional circumference 40,007.9 km = 24,859.7 miles
Equatorial circumference 40,075.0 km = 24,901.4 miles
Mean circumference 40,041.4 km = 24,880.6 miles

The meridional circumference is sometimes called the polar circumference because it is a measure around the Earth going through the North and South poles.

In The Lost Science of Measuring the Earth, the authors claim that the "geodetic basis of ancient measures" is 24,883.2 miles. Comparing this value of the Earth's circumference with the mean value given by WGS84, yields an accuracy of 99.99%. The Earth's diameter of 7920 miles x 864/275 (an ancient approximation of Pi which encodes the number of the Sun) = 24,883.2 miles.

Michell and Heath go on to show how numerous ancient units of measure are grouped into families related to 24,883.2 miles by whole number multipliers. Two such examples are 86,400,000 Greek cubits (of 1.52064 feet) and 108,000,000 Roman remen (of 1.216512 feet) which each equal 24,883.2 miles exactly. Notice how 864 and 108 are encoded into the multipliers; these are the numbers of the Sun and Moon, respectively.

In Chapter 4 - The Honeycomb and the Apple, I discuss the deep relationship of 6 to 5 and profile many of the ways 6/5 is a harmonic structure of reality. Without getting into that discussion yet, let us take 6/5, or 1.2 when written as a decimal, as an elemental unit of measure.

To form a practical measure from this elemental measure we will imagine a cube with edge length 6/5. We must *cube it* (there is no etymological connection I am aware of but there is this synchronicity) to embody the canonical Egyptian cubit. The cubit is traditionally represented in the human body as the distance from the elbow to the tip of the middle finger. Cubes are symbols of embodiment, and cubing the elemental relationship in some way gives volume and life to the practical measure.

Cubing 6/5 means multiplying (6/5) x (6/5) x (6/5) or raising (6/5) to the third power which is written as: $(6/5)^3$. In decimal form this is 1.2 x 1.2 x 1.2 = 1.728

We are left with a cubit of exactly 1.728 but what are its units? John Neal's <u>All Done with Mirrors: an Exploration of Measure, Proportion, Ratio, and Number</u> (Secret Academy 2000) confirms that the English foot is the root of ancient measurement systems. Neal shows how various units of ancient measure are related by fractions such that all the units together constitute an integrated global system of measure that was obviously designed at some unknown point in the distant past.

The following graphic shows the fractional relationships between ancient Egyptian units of measure and the "English" foot. For example, 1 English foot times 8/7 equals 1.142857142857... which is the ancient Egyptian foot. The horizontal lines above numerals indicate sequences of digits that repeat forever. 441/440 is the relation of the Earth's mean radius to the polar radius and 176/175 allows for Earth's equatorial bulge. These units were designed to be used at different latitudes to measure temples and distances on the Earth. After all, the word *geometry* means Earth measure, used to dimension temples and to measure distances on the Earth.

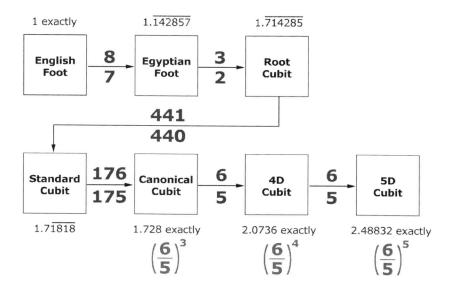

The values in parentheses at the bottom of the diagram are multipliers related directly to the English foot. For example, 1 foot times $(6/5)^3$ = 1.728 feet exactly (the canonical cubit). I have contributed the last two units, which I have named the 4D cubit and 5D cubit for reasons that will soon become clear.

In 1637 John Greaves made a survey of the Great Pyramid more accurate than any traveler that had preceded him. Greaves came to the unlikely conclusion that the English foot was at the root of the metrology of the Great Pyramid.

A generation later, Isaac Newton wrote in his <u>Dissertation Upon the Sacred Cubit of the Jews and the Cubits of Several Nations</u> that a certain cubit of Memphis was 1.727 English feet. He was off from what Neal called the "canonical Egyptian cubit" of 1.728 feet by only one part in a thousand.

I realized that the canonical cubit could be arrived at more directly from the English foot than multiplying 8/7 x 3/2 x 441/440 x 176/175 by simply raising 6/5 to the third power.

I raised 6/5 to the fourth and fifth powers and discovered hyper-dimensional encoding embodied by the Great Pyramid, the precise mean size of the Earth, and the latitude of Memphis, Egypt.

$$\left(\frac{6}{5}\right)^3 = 1.728' = 20.736''$$

CANONICAL EGYPTIAN CUBE-IT

$$\left(\frac{6}{5}\right)^4 = 2.0736' = 24.8832''$$

EARTH'S MEAN CIRCUM = 24,883.2 MILES

$$\left(\frac{6}{5}\right)^5 = 2.48832' = 29.85984''$$

LATITUDE OF MEMPHIS, EGYPT = 29.85984°N

The 4D Cubit reveals a resonance between the number of inches in the unit and the number of miles in the Earth's mean circumference.

The 5D Cubit reveals a resonance between the number of inches in the unit and the decimal latitude of Memphis.

There is added symmetry in what Newton called the cubit of Memphis being two dimensions below the encoding of the latitude of Memphis itself.

Memphis marks the boundary between upper and lower Egypt. Memphis was once the capital of Egypt and was for centuries the largest settlement worldwide.

Sadly, there is almost nothing left of ancient Memphis today. Perhaps now we know why Memphis was located where it was, and have a greater appreciation for how seriously the ancient Egyptians took the phrase, *"all is number,"* a phrase that their student Pythagoras later echoed in his famous dictum.

The 4D cubit of 24.8832 inches resonates with the Earth's mean circumference of 24,883.2 miles by virtue of our units of measure.

If there weren't exactly 12 inches in a foot or 5280 feet in a mile then this resonance would not occur.

The Earth's mean circumference can be arrived at directly by multiplying 12^4 by 6/5. In other words:

24,883.2 miles = 12 x 12 x 12 x 12 x (6/5)

Raising 12 to the fourth power is in some sense a higher dimensional act. Poetically speaking, the mean circumference of the Earth is found within a 4D zodiac (12^4) as a crossroads between macrocosm (6) and microcosm (5).

In summary, I've presented four independent systems entangling inches, feet, furlongs, miles, ancient Egyptian units, angular measure, geographic measure, the mean circumference of the Earth, the Earth's orbital period, the distance from the Sun to the Earth, the decimal system, and the speed of light in a hyper-dimensional web of number.

The mind behind the design of the units that we call the inch, foot, furlong, and mile is clearly light years ahead of us. It is a wonder that many of these systems are still in use so that they are fresh and accessible to all people today.

The Sacredness of the Meter

Born in revolutionary France in 1793, the metric system has taken little more than 200 years to spread across the world. The strongest resistance to metrication has come from the US, and to a much lesser extent the UK, which is officially metric but where the population still clings to some Imperial units. Aside from the US, Myanmar, and Liberia, all the other countries in the world have officially adopted the International System of Units (SI in French).

One-world-units have streamlined international trade and made scientific calculations much easier. So it is not surprising how this monoculture of units has dominated the world. The number of people who are aware of the wisdom encoded into the system of inches, feet, cubits, furlongs, and miles is a very tiny minority.

Considering the politics, you might assume that the push for metrication is a conspiracy to wipe out the wisdom encoded in the ancient system of measurement discussed in the previous section.

This is a definite possibility. However, you might be surprised to learn that the meter is actually a unit with ancient provenance, contrary to popular belief.

John Charles Webb, Jr. discovered that the latitude of the Great Pyramid (GP) encodes the speed of light in meters per second.

The speed of light is 299,792,458 meters/second.
The latitude of GP is 29.9792458 degrees north of the equator.

This correlation alone speaks volumes. Sadly, most people reflexively dismiss facts that don't fit into accepted conventional frameworks saying things like "Primitive people who worshipped animal-headed gods could never have known the speed of light, have been using metric units, or been able to locate anything with GPS coordinates."

No matter the logic or the rhetoric, the fact remains that the GP's position encodes the speed of light.

By studying the Trivium (see http://triviumeducation.com) one learns not to put logic before grammar and to leave off the rhetoric until first grammar and then logic have been satisfied. In other words first gather the facts by asking Who? What? When? and Where? (the grammar) and see if you can hold off on definitively supplying the logic of Why and ultimately persuading people as to the rhetoric of How until the grammar is fully collected. If we put rhetoric or logic first it interferes with and can dramatically restrict our ability to assimilate the grammar.

Without the proper grammar the uncritical thinker's logic is necessarily flawed and their rhetoric hollow. The foundation of critical thinking is processing grammar, logic, and rhetoric in that order.

Consider a new piece of grammar I discovered:

Earth's polar circumference is 6/5 x 33,333,333 meters (99.98%).

Logically the meter must be a resonant measure in order to encode such elegant and fundamental numerical relationships.

The meter must either be an ancient measure known to the designers of the GP who selected its site to encode the speed of light (c), or the metric system was designed post hoc to encode the speed of light in the location of the GP.

The problem with the former hypothesis is it presupposes the ancient Egyptians not only could measure latitude with extremely high accuracy but that they also had an accurate value of **c** in meters/second. The problem with the latter hypothesis is that it presupposes the 18th century French knew **c** with enough accuracy to encode the precise location of the GP using the meter. The history of science shows that **c** wasn't known with sufficient accuracy until the 20th century.

This situation reveals an advanced knowledge that is out of place according to conventional explanations. However, before jumping to the conclusion that ancient aliens are the cause (they might indeed be, but ancient aliens is but one of many possibilities), more grammar must be collected and sifted. Jump ahead to Chapter 9 - Behind the Curtain if you can't wait for speculations on who might have designed the metric system and much else besides, but then come back here and continue assimilating the grammar.

In Livio C. Stecchini's <u>A History of Measures</u> (1971), he writes about Julius Oppert (1825–1905) and "his decisive contribution to the discovery of the Sumerian language and Sumerian culture." Stecchini continues:

Oppert's monumental and epoch-making study of the culture of cuneiform-writing nations includes about thirty articles dealing with measures. These articles are still today an inspiring model of correct methodology in dealing with Mesopotamian metrics...Oppert tried to find a confirmation of his reckoning by applying Newton's method which had been so successful in Egypt. He devoted himself to the interpretation of architectural measurements and also, following Newton's suggestion, assumed that the size of most bricks would be in simple numerical relation with the unit of length...

From the size of bricks he concluded that the Mesopotamian foot has a value of circa 330 mm. (it is in reality a barley foot of 333 mm), but later he hesitated because he found evidence of a foot of 315 mm (in reality a wheat foot of 314.5 mm)

The basic units of length in the Sumerian and Akkadian cultures include the following measures:

Wheat Foot 0.315 meters (recalling Pi)
Barley Foot 0.333 meters
Step 1.000 meters
Reed 3.000 meters
Rod 6.000 meters
Cord 60.000 meters

Ancient Mesopotamian units of measure (http://bit.ly/R0UFSL) appear to be based on what we call the metric system.

One mile is Phi kilometers (99%). By connecting the mile and the kilometer via the golden ratio, the measures are linked by perhaps the most interesting mathematical relationship of all time. In The Golden Ratio: The Story of Phi, The World's Most Astonishing Number (Broadway 2002), Mario Livio writes:

Some of the greatest mathematical minds of all ages, from Pythagoras and Euclid in ancient Greece, through the medieval Italian mathematician Leonardo of Pisa and the Renaissance astronomer Johannes Kepler, to present-day scientific figures such as Oxford physicist Roger Penrose, have spent endless hours over this simple ratio and its properties. But the fascination with the Golden Ratio is not confined just to mathematicians. Biologists, artists, musicians, historians, architects, psychologists, and even mystics have pondered and debated the basis of its ubiquity and appeal. In fact, it is probably fair to say that the Golden Ratio has inspired thinkers of all disciplines like no other number in the history of mathematics.

The distance from Glastonbury Tor to Avebury ring is 66,666 meters. Consider also that the distance between Stonehenge and Silbury Hill is 86,400 feet. Were Neolithic tribespeople encoding distances in meters and feet in the selection of their temple sites? Did they know the diameter of the Sun in miles? My approach is to entertain these possibilities and remain open minded to other explanations as well.

In Before the Pyramids (Watkins 2011) Christopher Knight and Alan Butler show that the outer two of the three henges of Thornborough, UK are 1500 meters apart on center, suggesting they were laid out using the meter. Incidentally the three henges of Thornborough perfectly mirror the belt of Orion, just like the three pyramids of Giza do as Robert Bauval and Adrian Gilbert pointed out in <u>The Orion Mystery</u> (Doubleday 1994).

In <u>Before the Pyramids,</u> Knight and Butler made an important correlation between the meter and the second by using a pendulum (a weight that can swing back and forth, hung from a fixed pivot point). The length from the weight to the pivot point controls every pendulum's period of oscillation. When a pendulum is one meter long it will swing with a period of 1 second in each direction (99%).

The length of a meter has a relationship to how we divide the Earth's rotation into 86,400 seconds per mean solar day, and how this number is an order of magnitude below the Sun's diameter of 864,000 miles (99.9%).

In 1675 Tito Burattini proposed that the length of the seconds pendulum be called the *Catholic meter*, more than a century before the meter was codified in France. Interestingly, Burattini explored the Great Pyramid with John Greaves and reported to the Jesuit Athanasius Kircher, who you'll read more about later.

A connection spanning five millennia can be seen in the distance between Silbury Hill and the Shard. The distance between the tallest prehistoric human-made mound in Europe and the tallest modern building in the European Union is 123,456 meters.

The distance between Notre Dame de Paris and Rosslyn Chapel is 864 kilometers. Both structures predate the International System of Units by hundreds of years. It is especially interesting that Rosslyn's distance from Notre Dame resonates with the Sun's 864,000 mile diameter (99.9%). Here again we have both meters and miles resonating with a key number.

I can think of no better place to alchemically relate Rosslyn to than Notre Dame de Paris, just as the Sun relates to the Moon.

Our Lady of Paris rides on the Ile de la Cite, which resembles the boat of Isis cutting through the Seine. The word *Paris* can be traced to Pharia-Isis according to Graham Hancock and Robert Bauval's research in <u>Talisman: Sacred Cities, Secret Faith</u> (Anchor Canada 2005). Pharia (Pharos in Greek) is the name of the island where the Lighthouse of Alexandria once stood. Stella Maris, or star of the sea, was an epithet for Isis. The Coat of Arms (from 1111 AD) of the City of Paris depicts a boat, perhaps because Paris itself was founded on the Ile de la Cité.

In Secrets In Plain Sight - Volume 1, I detailed the Grand Arch in Paris, which has 40,000 square meters of office space and multiple 400 square meter multi-purpose rooms in the basement. Twelve columns support the structure and a zodiac is literally depicted in the basement floor.

The meter is 1/40,000,000 the polar circumference of the Earth (99.98%)
The Moon is 1/400th the diameter of the Sun (99.8%)
The Moon is 1/400th of the distance from the Sun to the Earth (97%)

Just as the form of the Grand Arch is a 3D projection of a 4D hypercube, the way that the inch, foot, cubit, furlong, mile, meter, kilometer, and second relate to the Earth, Moon, Sun, and the speed of light is truly hyper-dimensional.

None of the aforementioned units of measure are arbitrary, but instead brilliantly encode the harmonics of reality for those who have eyes to see and the courage to contemplate the implications of what this all means.

Seeing multiple units encoded in the dimensions of a building, in the location of a temple on the Earth, or in the distance between significant sites are therefore all valid points of grammar, collected in an attempt to understand more about the material and numerical structures forming our reality.

Chapter 3 - Measuring Time

People like us, who believe in physics, know that the distinction between past, present, and future is only a stubbornly persistent illusion. -Albert Einstein

To quantify this illusion called time we have watched sand pass through the hourglass, swung pendulums, squeezed quartz crystals to produce piezoelectric pulses, and measured the radiation regularly emitted by caesium-133 atoms. However the surest and oldest time keeping method is to observe day turning into night and night into day, noticing the seasons change and repeat, tracking phases of the moon, and recording the slow precession of the fixed stars over many human lifetimes.

Is time an arrow flying from past, present, to the future or is time a circle, a spiral, or a web?

Are space and time one and the same fabric, with warp of space and weft of time? Is our imperfect perception of time really a glimpse of a fourth spatial dimension?

Fish have trouble seeing the water they swim in. We don't really know what time is. The wise say there is only the eternal now.

Nevertheless we measure days by dividing them into hours, minutes, and seconds. In a period of 24 hours (technically a mean solar day), with 60 minutes per hour, and 60 seconds per minute, there are exactly 86,400 seconds.

The ancient Egyptian year was divided into 36 *decans*, or periods of 10 days, plus 5 added festival days at the end of the year. (36 x 10) + 5 = 365.

One decan is 10 days x 86,400 seconds/day = 864,000 seconds.

Isn't it clever that the year, which is simply the Earth's motion around the Sun, would be divided into decans which mirror the Sun's diameter of 864,000 miles (99.9%). This presupposes synchronization between seconds and the mile.

Time is personified by Father Time, the deathly old man with the scythe. This image derives from the Grim Reaper and Chronos, the Greek god of time. Chronos is also associated with the titan Cronus who is usually depicted with a scythe. The Romans called this god

Saturn. All of these gods are echoes of Osiris, the ancient Egyptian Lord of the Dead.

The Sothic Calendar

The ancient Egyptians based their new year on the phenomenon of the heliacal rising of Sirius, star of Isis. This occurs on the first morning of the year when Sirius is visible on the Eastern horizon just before the Sun rises.

Jim Alison discovered that Pennsylvania Ave in Washington DC, which runs from the White House to the Capitol, is aligned to the heliacal rising of Sirius (see http://bit.ly/RaQmFX). This is a significant avenue of power, and a great secret in plain sight.

Robert Bauval and Graham Hancock showed in Talisman that the Champs-Elysees, which runs along the historical axis of Paris, is likewise oriented to the heliacal rising of Sirius and that the axis of Notre Dame de Paris is also thus aligned.

The Greek name for Sirius is Sothis. The Sothic cycle is a period of 1461 ancient Egyptian years of 365 days each. Because the ancient Egyptian year does not account for the extra approximate quarter day in the Earth's revolution about the Sun (365.242 days in the solar year), the date of the heliacal rising shifts throughout the year over time.

After a period of exactly 1461 years the date of the heliacal rising of Sirius returns to its original date. The original date is reckoned to be the summer solstice, the time of year when the Nile traditionally began its annual flood (before the Aswan dam was built in the 1960s which ended the flooding).

There are interesting parallels between ancient Egyptian time and ancient Olympic time. The summer Olympics were in ancient times and are again in modern times held every 4 years. In every 4 year period there are 4 x 365 days plus 1 extra day to account for leap day. Doing the math yields 1461 days. The Olympic period is 1461 days and the Sothic cycle is 1461 years. The frequency of Olympic games (and US Presidential elections for that matter) echoes the Sothic calendar.

In a blog called Groupname for Grapejuice, the writer recognized the following important connections between Sothic and Olympic time (see http://bit.ly/PFCJKW).

Sirius disappears for 70 days below the horizon immediately prior to its heliacal rising. The Egyptians equated this 70 day period with the journey of the soul through the Duat or underworld. This was echoed in the 70 day mummification process.

In preparation for the 2012 London summer Olympics, the torch was lit in Athens with a parabolic mirror from the light of the Sun. The Olympic torch began its relay in the UK at Land's End in Cornwall on May 19th, 70 days before the cauldron of 204 separate flames (referencing the 24 hours in a day) was lit at the opening ceremony on July 27th.

The torch relay covered a distance of 8000 miles, crisscrossing all over Britain to make up the required distance. The torch was carried by 8000 torchbearers and 8000 holes perforate each triangular torch. The diameter of the Earth is 8000 miles (99%). The torch relay thus represents a journey through the center of the Earth.

Dante's Divine Comedy (published circa 1310) has 3 books: Hell, Purgatory, and Paradise. Dante's journey through the Earth began in Jerusalem and passed through all the nine rings of Hell. Was Dante really describing the Egyptian underworld, complete with a reference to the ennead in the rings? Every night Ra takes the Sun on his boat through the Duat, facing many perils and monsters.

I noticed that each of Dante's books consists of exactly 33 cantos. Scientists at Stanford University recently discovered that the Sun's core rotates once every 33 days (http://bit.ly/dcykJ2).

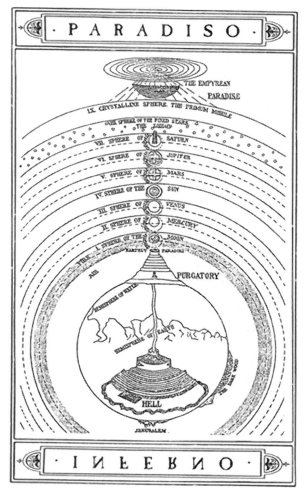

The 2012 London Olympics ended on August 12th and the Olympic flame was extinguished. The very next morning at the latitude of the London Olympic Stadium, the heliacal rising of Sirius signaled the beginning of another ancient Egyptian solar year. Is this all coincidence?

A Year and a Day (or Two)

There are modern echoes of an ancient tradition in which "a year and a day" was a significant period of time. In Wicca, a modern pagan religion, candidates must study for a year and a day before they are allowed to be formally initiated. In common law, there is a standard that death cannot be legally attributed to acts or omissions that occurred more than a year and a day before the death (this rule was codified in New Zealand's Crimes Act). In <u>Sacred Number and the Origins of Civilization</u> (Inner Traditions 2007) Robin Heath's brother Richard traced the tradition of a king ruling for "a year and a day", after which he was killed, back to the matriarchal societies of the Bronze Age.

"A year and a day" resonates with the ancient 13-month solar calendar, which had 13 equal months each composed of 28 days as 13 x 28 = 364. If 364 days comprise a year then one needs an extra festival day to equal the Sothic calendar of 365 days.

The International Fixed Calendar uses this 13-month solar calendar with one or two days added that are out-of-time, belonging to no month or week (called Year Day and Leap Day). This calendar has the distinct advantages of being a perennial calendar such that every date is always fixed on the same weekday and every month has equal length of four 7-day weeks. The 13th month, called Sol, is inserted between June and July at midsummer. Perhaps surprisingly, the International Fixed Calendar was the official calendar of the Eastman Kodak Company from 1928-1989.

Ophiucus, the serpent bearer, is the 13th constellation that crosses the ecliptic. In the "year and a day" 13 month calendar, the ancients would have required 13 zodiac signs corresponding more or less to the months. In <u>Babylonian Star Lore</u> (Solaria 2008), Gavin White proposes that the 13th zodiac sign Ophiuchus may in fact be remotely descended from a Babylonian constellation representing Nirah, a serpent-god who was sometimes depicted with his upper half human but with serpents for legs.

When the patriarchal cultures took over in the Iron Age the serpent was vilified, the calendar was changed to 12 months, and Ophiucus was largely forgotten.

Ophiucus is located between Sagittarius and Scorpio on the ecliptic. The arrow of Sagittarius and the stinger of Scorpio both reach toward Ophiucus' foot that is trampling the scorpion. The convergence of these symbols just happens to point in the direction of our galactic core at the intersection of the ecliptic and the galactic mid-plane, which is also symbolized as the golden gate, or gate of death. See my Esoteric Astronomy episode in Secrets In Plain Sight - Volume 1 for more information.

Perhaps Eve learned all this when she ate the apple from the Tree of Knowledge proffered by the serpent. Adam and Eve's expulsion from the garden by Yahweh, which also vilified femininity and the serpent, seems to me to be related to dropping Ophiucus. Tracing the astronomical origins of religious stories is known as *astrotheology*. Santos Bonacci (http://universaltruthschool.com) is a master of this "holy science."

John Michell's New Jerusalem diagram in <u>The Dimensions of Paradise: Sacred Geometry, Ancient Science, and the Heavenly Order on Earth</u> (Inner Traditions 2008) resonates with the concept of "a year and a day." Its 13 months are symbolized by the smaller circles, the 28 points of four 7-pointed stars represent the days and weeks of the months. The larger Earth circle behind the stars represents the extra day. The diagram is created by squaring the circle and the large Earth circle and smaller months/moon circles are in the proper proportion of 3:11.

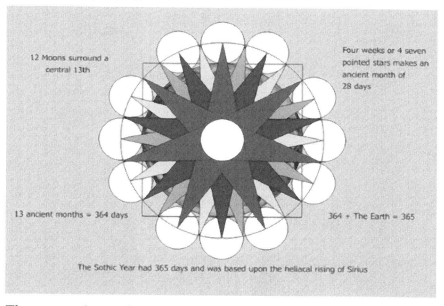

The numerology of playing cards also encodes "a year and a day." There are 4 suits corresponding to the seasons, or 2 solstices (black) and 2 equinoxes (red). There are 13 cards in each suit (Ace through 10 plus 3 royals), corresponding to the months in the year. The 12 face cards correspond to the months of the solar year. Adding the face values of each suit:

$1+2+3+4+5+6+7+8+9+10+11+12+13 = 91$.

Totaling the values of all suits, $4 \times 91 = 364$. Therefore the total face values of the cards correspond to the days in the year. The Jokers are Year Day and optionally Leap Day making up the Sothic or Gregorian year, respectively.

The Gregorian calendar that we use today alternates between a 365 and 366 day year to compensate for the Earth's actual solar year of 365.242 days. In this calendar the following rules determine whether a year will have 365 days or 366 days.

Every fourth year will generally be a leap year when we have a February 29th, except every 100 years there won't be a leap year (i.e. 1900 AD wasn't a leap year). Also every 400 years we skip the exception (i.e. 2000 AD was a leap year). And every 4000 years we will also have to remember to skip leap year (i.e. 4000 AD won't be a leap year). Got that?

Looking back, when the Gregorian calendar started in 1582 AD, it began by skipping 10 days to restore the vernal equinox to March 21st. This remains a challenging problem when trying to calculate exactly how many days ago something happened when the Gregorian calendar crosses into the previous Julian calendar (in addition to the complexity of keeping track of Gregorian leap days).

The Gregorian calendar we use today is officially called the "current or Common Era" and this is abbreviated CE. Dates before the Common Era are abbreviated BCE. The older acronyms AD and BC are considered politically incorrect because AD stands for the Latin *Anno Domini Nostri Iesu Christi*, which means "In the Year of Our Lord Jesus Christ."

The attention given to being supposedly politically correct by using CE/BCE rather than AD/BC is a triviality that distracts people from the fact that our global calendar is still based on Jesus Christ no matter which abbreviation you use. Perhaps we are still basing time on Jesus Christ because today 33% of the world's population is Christian, 21% are Muslim, 14% are non-religious, 13% are Hindu, 12% belong to many other religions, 6% are Buddhist, and just 0.2% are Jewish.

The English acronym BC means "Before Christ", so many

reasonably but mistakenly assume AD means "After Death," rather than an acronym standing for the phrase, "In the Year [since the birth] of Our Lord Jesus Christ." Further confusion about this concept stems from the problem of deciding when the year 1 AD was supposed to have been. The Gregorian calendar places Christ's birth on Dec 25th, 1 AD. Christ lived approximately 33-1/3 years, so that his death came at Easter in 35 AD.

There is no year zero in the calendar, so 5 BC was 9 years before 5 AD. The years follow this pattern: 2 BC, 1 BC 1 AD, 2 AD, etc. It is very confusing accounting for exactly how many years ago something happened before the Common Era. Of course it is also very confusing counting backwards in the whole BC epoch. For example, Julius Caesar was born in 100 BC and died in 44 BC at the age of 55 years.

If civilization is ever interrupted it seems unlikely that anyone will remember all the complexities, exceptions, and peculiarities of the Gregorian calendar. However, even this tortured calendar resonates with the phrase "a year and a day" as 52 weeks x 7 days = 364 days.

I would hope the simplicity of the 13 month fixed calendar will eventually supplant our current convoluted system of variable length months, shifting days and dates, and month names prefixed with Sept which means 7, Oct which means 8, Nov which means 9, and Dec which means 10, all being out of phase with the year. We have Julius (July) and Augustus (August) Caesar to thank for our collective dissociation with time. Perhaps our global calendar was a Roman plan to divide and conquer the mind in time? This appears to have worked very well.

The Lunar Year

The Muslim calendar is a purely lunar calendar consisting of 12 lunar months of 354 or 355 days (based on the lunar synodic year of 354.367 days). A lunar month is the average period of the Moon's revolution with respect to a line joining the Sun and Earth, which turns out to be 29.5 days. This is the period of one full moon to the next.

The Muslim calendar is not synchronized with the Sun and thus seasons drift over time by about 11 days a year. The Muslim calendar gets synchronized with the solar year every 33 Muslim years.

The first year in the Muslim calendar was 622 AD when Muhammad moved from Mecca to Medina. The current Muslim year is 1433 in the year of the Hijra (which equates to the year 2012 AD in the Gregorian calendar). The Muslim calendar is the official calendar of Saudi Arabia.

*****

In The Lost Science of Measuring the Earth, John Michell and Robin Heath identified a 5:12:13 Pythagorean triangle that forms a greater temple around Stonehenge that I described in Secrets In Plain Sight - Volume 1. Lundy Island is the right angle point of the triangle, with Stonehenge due East, and due north the quarry in the Preseli hills of Wales where the bluestones used in Stonehenge were mined.

There are 12 months in the solar year but 13 resonates with the Moon. Most years have 12 full moons but every second or third year has 13. The Moon's dance with the Sun is complicated. Calculating the date of Easter, which is tied to both the Moon and the Sun, is a kind of calendrical rocket science.

The most harmonious interval in any dance is the musical fifth. If this tone is struck it forms a just 3:2 interval. Michell and Heath drew a line from Stonehenge to the 3:2 point on the line between Lundy and Preseli and discovered that not only does it go to a giant menhir on Caldey Island that a priory church is built around, but its proportion measures 12.369 which is the number of full moons in a year (99.99%). This is also the square root of the number 153 (to 5 significant digits), which has esoteric, religious, and architectural significance, see Key Numbers.

The Sidereal Year

A solar year is 365.242 days but the Earth actually rotates 366 times a year relative to the fixed stars. A *sidereal* (with respect to distant stars) day is 236 seconds less than a mean solar day. The subtle discrepancy between the solar and sidereal day is caused by the curvature of the Earth's orbit. Over the year this difference amounts to the Earth rotating one extra day relative to the stars.

We have already seen the number 366 used as the number of days in a leap year.

Consider also that the Earth is 366.6% the size of the Moon.

The Lunisolar Year

Lunisolar calendars incorporate the movements of both Moon and Sun in their earthly timekeeping. This complicated relationship produces calendars requiring complex intercalation, or insertion of days, weeks, and/or months to make the math work out. Many traditional Asian calendars are lunisolar. Interestingly, the calculation of Easter is not tied to the Gregorian calendar because it is lunisolar.

The Jewish calendar is also lunisolar—it indicates both the moon phase and season of the solar year. The Jewish calendar is tied to the Metonic cycle, a 19-year period that more or less synchronizes the Moon with the Sun. The Jewish calendar is the official calendar of Israel. It started *Anno Mundi* or "at the creation of the world" in 3760 BC.

The year 2013 AD is the Jewish year 5773 AM.

Here's a timely correlation: the Great Pyramid is 5773 inches in height.

Richard Heath offered the following metrology in Sacred Number and the Origins of Civilization. The Great Pyramid is 1/11th of a mile (480 feet) in height for what is called the *unfinished pyramid,* plus a 1-1/11 foot high *pyramidion* to cap it off. 481.1 feet is 5773 inches.

There are a total of 2013 minutes in 33°33'.

The square root of 33.33 is approximately 5.773.

The Circle of the Year

Compared to the complexity of lunisolar schemes, a far simpler approach to timekeeping is to average the apparent motions of the Earth and Moon about the Sun. The Earth's solar synodic year is 365.242 days and the lunar synodic year is 354.367 days. Adding these periods and dividing by 2 yields an average of 360 days, to three significant figures.

Robert Temple wrote in <u>The Crystal Sun</u> (Century 2000):

I divided the duration of the Earth's year which is 365.242392, by 360...and wondered what the relationship between the two numbers could be. I was very surprised when I saw that the result was 1.014562, for I instantly recognized that it was the same (99.9%) as the Comma of Pythagoras to the third decimal place.

I mentioned the Comma earlier in Chapter 2 - Metrology.

The ancient Persians used a 360-day calendar based on the Babylonian division of the circle into 360 degrees. This calendar is a beautiful marriage between circular angular measure and the annual cycle. It is easy to visualize where you are in the course of a circular 360-day year. The Celtic calendar is based on the equal division of the year into 8 parts, making a solar symbol in the process.

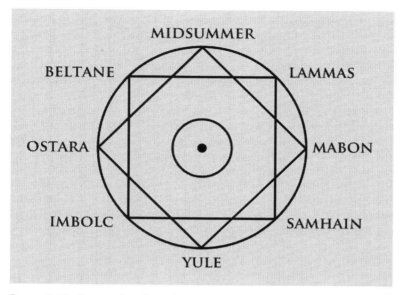

In a 360-day calendar the solstices and equinoxes are 90 days apart, analogous to how a right angle measures 90 degrees in a circle. The circle of the year makes a lot of sense.

William Neil pointed out the following parallels in <u>How We Were Made</u>, (Oracle Books 2010):

360 feet = 4320 inches.
The Sun's radius is 432000 miles (99.8%).

360 yards = 1080 feet.
The Moon's radius is 1080 miles (99.9%).

1080 feet = 12960 inches.
The Earth's precession period is traditionally reckoned to be 2 x 12960 years.

*****

The Mayan Tun is a period of 360 days in the Tzolkin (long count) calendar. Even today, the 360-day calendar is utilized in a variety of modeling software to measure durations in modern financial markets.

However, the 360-day year is out of phase with the seasons. It needs to be adjusted with the addition of 6 days on leap year or 5 days on a regular year to keep in sync with our solar year. I think it is especially interesting that the gap would be precisely 6 or 5 days (see The Honeycomb and the Apple).

The ancient Egyptian, modern Coptic (12 months of 30 days each), and French Republican calendars all use or used a 360 day year that has 6 or 5 days tacked on which are not part of any decan, decade, or month in order to sync up with the solar year.

In my reading of myth I speculate that the Earth once had an orbital period of exactly 360 days in the "golden age." There were no seasons then because the celestial equator was more or less parallel to the ecliptic. Therefore, the weather was constant with equal days and nights and humans lived in a lush equatorial "garden of Eden" where plants that are now annuals were probably then perennials. You can imagine why it was called a paradisiacal garden!

Whether due to comets striking or exploding above the Earth's surface, a near miss by what became the planet Venus according to Immanuel Velikovsky's Worlds in Collision (Dell 1950), or an advanced antediluvian technology gone wrong, the Earth's axis was cataclysmically tilted resulting in what we now experience as seasons.

After the cataclysm our orbital path was expanded slightly, making the year 365.242 days. The English foot must have been defined after the cataclysm because as I pointed out earlier, the number of feet in the Earth's equatorial circumference is 365.242 x 360,000 (99.99%).

In the cataclysm much of the ice melted causing the Great Flood, and as the massive loading of water on the planet shifted from North America and Europe to the Atlantic basin, Atlantis sunk and most of civilization was drowned by the now much higher global sea level.

The Great Year

The Earth rotates on its axis once every day and of course revolves around the Sun every year but there is a much longer cycle called the *Great Year*. Noticing this longer cycle requires record keeping over many generations because its period is so long. In fact, the average human life span is approximately one day in the Great Year.

To understand the Great Year, you need a few simple astronomy fundamentals under your belt. The apparent path that the Sun takes through the stars is called the ecliptic. The planets (Mercury, Venus, Mars, etc) appear to travel along the ecliptic because this is the plane in which these planets and the Earth orbit the Sun. The stars along the ecliptic are grouped into constellations called the zodiac (Aries, Taurus, Gemini, etc).

Astronomers and navigators have for millennia imagined a transparent celestial sphere surrounding the Earth at some arbitrary large scale. The Earth's equator is projected outward onto the celestial sphere and this is called the celestial equator. The fixed stars are also imagined to be projected downward onto the surface of this transparent celestial sphere.

The celestial equator is currently tilted 23.4 degrees with respect to the ecliptic. This tilt causes the seasons as the Earth travels along its orbit around the Sun.

William Neil noticed the following interesting numbers arising from the Earth's tilt angle (also known as the obliquity) of 23.4 degrees:

The Tropic of Cancer is 66.6 degrees from the North pole (90 - 23.4 = 66.6) and the Tropic of Capricorn is similarly 66.6 degrees from the South Pole.

The Arctic and Antarctic circles are 66.6 degrees from the Equator.
The Earth's average orbital speed is 66,666 miles per hour (99.9%).

The Sun is in the same plane as the celestial equator on exactly two days a year: the equinoxes, when day and night have equal length. We have vernal and autumnal equinoxes around March 20 and Sept 22, respectively.

Over many generations, observers noticed that the Sun was slipping backward through zodiac signs on the equinoxes. This slip is retrograde (backwards) to the direction the Sun moves every day through the zodiac. However the slip is so slow that it literally takes an age (approximately two millennia) to move from one sign to the preceding zodiac sign. The phenomenon is called the *Precession of the Equinoxes*. We are currently nearing the end of the age of Pisces and "it is the dawning of the Age of Aquarius." The entire cycle of the precession of the equinoxes is called the Great Year.

Traditionally, the equinoxes have been reckoned to precess about 1 degree every 72 years. Therefore 72 years x 360 degrees = 25,920 years which is the traditional period of the Great Year.

Neil also noticed that the New Jerusalem described in St. John's revelatory vision encodes some interesting numbers relating to the Great Year:

And the city lieth foursquare, and the length is as large as the breadth: and he measured the city with the reed, twelve thousand furlongs. The length and the breadth and the height of it are equal.
-Revelation 21:16

The new Jerusalem describes a cube having a volume of 12,000 furlongs cubed which equals 1.728×10^{12} cubic furlongs.

Amazingly there are exactly 66,666,666.666... Great Years in 1.728×10^{12} years. Recall that a furlong is 660 feet. That is a lot of sixes to be just a coincidence.

Dividing 25,920 by 12 to find the number of years per zodiacal sign yields 2,160 years per age. It is interesting that the Moon's diameter is 2160 miles (99.9%) because that numerologically corroborates that an age, or month, of the Great Year resonates with our Moon. The Greek word *mene* (moon) is the root of the English words moon, month, and menstruation. Again we see how distance, as measured in miles, is synchronized with our Earth's orbital period measured in years through the digits 216. It is interesting that summer solstice in the Northern hemisphere and winter solstice in the Southern hemisphere occur on the 21st of June, or 21/6, and 216 = 6 x 6 x 6.

Sirius Does Not Precess

Walter Cruttenden (http://binaryresearchinstitute.com) has highlighted the salient fact that Sirius does not precess. He cites research done by physicist Jed Z. Buchwald and astronomer Karl-Heinz Homann revealing that the heliacal risings of Sirius stay phase-locked to the precession of the vernal point (the intersection of the celestial equator and the ecliptic) over thousands of years, while all the other stars in the sky slip slowly backward. The implications of this observation are staggering.

Cruttenden realized that this means our Sun is in a binary system with Sirius. Binary stars are gravitationally bound to each other and revolve around their common empty center of mass. NASA's Chandra website (http://chandra.harvard.edu) reports that more than 80% of all stars in the universe are in multiple star systems containing 2 or more stars. Why not ours?

Pardon the pun, but this is a revolution in thinking. I see the Cruttenden revolution as akin to the Copernican revolution in terms of what it will ultimately do for philosophy.

Just before his death, Nicolaus Copernicus published <u>De Revolutionibus Orbium Coelestium</u> (1542) with a heliocentric cosmology explaining how the planets orbit the Sun rather than the Earth. Our assumed position at the center of the universe was eventually dethroned and we grew intellectually as a species. However, at the time the Pope forced Galileo to recant and suffer the rest of his life under house arrest for publishing his telescope observations confirming Copernicus was correct.

Mathematics is the alphabet with which God has written the universe. -Galileo

Cruttenden's Binary Companion Theory explains that the cause of precession is our solar system's motion relative to Sirius. The current lunisolar theory in science textbooks attempts to explain precession as the Sun and Moon tugging on Earth's less than 1% equatorial bulge. There are numerous problems with the lunisolar model that Cruttenden systematically addresses and resolves with the Binary Companion Theory.

The Binary Companion Theory also elegantly explains why the precessional rate has been observed to be speeding up. Our systems follow elliptical paths in the binary arrangement so we accelerate as we come into closer proximity to our common center of mass and decelerate as we move away from it. Periapsis is the point where our systems are closest together and Apoapsis is the point where they are the farthest apart in the Great Year.

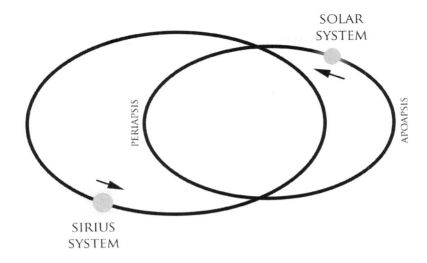

Thankfully, Cruttenden doesn't appear to be suffering the same fate as Galileo although most astronomers and astrophysicists haven't accepted the theory. The next generation will grow up with minds open to models that better describe the structure of reality. Thomas S. Kuhn's <u>Structure of Scientific Revolutions: 50th Anniversary Edition</u> (University of Chicago Press 2012) shows that this is in fact how scientific revolutions occur rather than via established scientists changing their opinions during their professional careers.

To me, one of the most interesting aspects of this mind-opening binary theory is of course the numbers. Cruttenden has found that the average period that best fits the data is a *24,000-year* cycle of precession.

Swami Sri Yukteswar (1855-1936) is probably best known as the great sage and teacher of Paramahansa Yogananda as written in his <u>Autobiography of a Yogi</u> (Self Realization Fellowship 1946). Yukteswar claimed that the Great Year is 24,000 years, and this was much later published in <u>The Holy Science </u>(Self-Realization Fellowship 1990). Through meditation he obtained not only self-realization (enlightenment) but also detailed scientific knowledge.

I have much to say about 24 in Key Numbers. 24 is a number that resonates with time, the precessional cycle, the Fibonacci sequence, Phi, and prime numbers, among other things.

The minimum precessional rate is 72 years per degree, which produces the traditional figure of 25,920 years for the full cycle. The rate of precession used to be 72 years per degree and will be again when our system reaches *apoapsis*, the greatest distance we reach from Sirius in our mutual orbits. The maximum precession rate will be 60 years per degree at periapsis. The relationship of the minimum to maximum rates of precession is 72:60 or 6:5.

The average rate of precession for the Great Year is *66.66 years per degree*.

Consider that the force that binds Sol and Sirius in a binary system is gravity. It turns out that Isaac Newton's gravitational constant is:

$G = 6.666 \times 10^{-11}$ cubic meters per kilogram second squared.

This new, more accurate measurement of Newton's gravitational constant was reported in the January 5, 2007 issue of Science ("Atom Interferometer Measurement of the Newtonian Constant of Gravity" (by J. B. Fixler, G. T. Foster, J. M. McGuirk, and M. A. Kasevich).

The value of $G = 6.666 \times 10^{-11}$ cubic meters per kilogram second squared fits within the narrow tolerance of standard error in the atom interferometer experiment and it is my opinion that this is the "correct" value, based on the repetitive single digits.

It is uncanny how distance, mass, and time as encoded in the gravitational constant resonate with repetitive single digits through SI units.

Isaac Newton was more of an alchemist than a scientist judging by how much he wrote on each subject. He tried to calculate G from the size of the Earth encoded in the dimensions of the Great Pyramid and Solomon's temple and was very close to discovering the key, but he was ultimately unsuccessful in this effort. The Great Pyramid does encode the size of the Earth through the number 432. See Number Patterns for this discussion.

Newton devised the first ever temperature scale (called Newtons) that went from 0 degrees for freezing ice to 33 degrees for boiling water. He seemed to know the significance of the key number 33 and would be probably be pleased with the repetitive single digits in the modern calculation of G.

Perhaps Gravitation is another definition of the freemasons' mysterious G at the center of their compasses and square emblem?

Sirius is the brightest star in our sky because it is so close, bound to our Sun in a binary relationship. How could we miss this until now? A tribe in Mali called the Dogon have known much about Sirius for thousands of years but we have largely ignored what they have had to say, assuming that their stories are just part of the "primitive" mythological imagination.

The Dogon

When Robert Temple published The Sirius Mystery (Sidgwick & Jackson 1976) it challenged belief systems because it revealed that the Dogon have preserved detailed astronomical knowledge that Sirius is actually itself a binary star that gravitationally binds together Sirius A (a bright star) and Sirius B (a dense dwarf star). This knowledge wasn't scientifically verified until modern times with the advent of powerful telescopes. The following question is well-worth considering, "How could the Dogon have known this?"

Laird Scranton has taken up the case in recent times and greatly expanded the discussion about the wisdom preserved by Dogon priests with the publication of his books The Science of the Dogon (2006), Sacred Symbols of the Dogon (2007), and The Cosmological Origins of Myth and Symbol (2010).

Scranton shows that the modern Dogon culture has numerous close parallels with pre-dynastic Egypt, going back before the invention of hieroglyphic writing. It appears that millennia ago a group of Dogon split off from Egypt, possibly from Nabta Playa in the south of Egypt and settled to the northwest in climatically inhospitable Mali, expressly to ensure the preservation of their knowledge through time.

The knowledge preserved by the black-skinned Dogon correlates with what Robert Bauval is saying in his fascinating book Black Genesis (Inner Traditions 2011). Namely that an advanced black-skinned tribe inhabited Nabta Playa long before Pharaonic Egypt and that they gave rise to the dynastic Egyptian civilization.

Dogon myths tell the story of how they were given the art and science of civilization by advanced beings they refer to as "teachers." Scranton shows that the Dogon word for teachers is phonetically the same as the Egyptian word for Sirius. Interestingly, the Dogon claim their teachers were spiritual rather than physical creatures. To me that suggests higher-dimensional communication rather than extra-terrestrial colonization.

Another Dogon story says eight Dogon individuals were chosen to be educated by the teachers and then these eight in turn educated the rest of their tribe. This is echoed in the Bible story of Noah, his wife, their 3 sons, and their wives being the sole survivors of the flood waters (4 men and 4 women).

The Dogon's myths and drawings encode much about the structure of reality that parallels what modern physicists have discovered about the atom, string theory, astronomy, and even biology. For example, Dogon drawings and stories have amazing parallels to genetics and sexual reproduction. This is the subject of Chapter 8 in Scranton's The Science of the Dogon.

After having my own mind opened to how the teachers' stories work on many levels, encoding scientific concepts that even the priests themselves might not be aware of, I made this visual connection between cell division and a 3,000 year old papyrus illustration of the ancient Egyptian creation myth. The myth begins with the world arising as a circular mound in an infinite sea. The sun is shown rising and setting with eight inherent primeval qualities of the water, represented as the 4 male and 4 female principles referred to as the Ogdoad. The Ogdoad correlates strongly with chromosomes' appearance in anaphase during cell mitosis. The creation myth encodes biological and cosmological concepts in a story people can understand and transmit through generations, even if they are not aware of all its levels of meaning.

 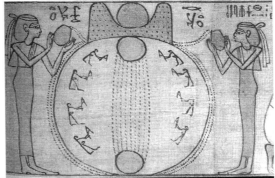

MITOSIS: CELL BIRTH   EGYPTIAN ZEP TEPI: SUNRISE AT CREATION

The birth of the cell (illustration on the left from <u>Gray's Anatomy</u>) has a striking resemblance to the mythological time of creation, called Zep Tepi. Scholars tend to dismiss parallels like this because they know that the ancient Egyptians did not posses the microscope so they logically assume that ancients could not have knowledge of the cell. Although I agree that it is unlikely that the ancient Egyptians were consciously aware of cell biology, they nevertheless appear to have been carriers of this knowledge via the complex encodings given to them by the teachers.

If the teachers are from Sirius, they would presumably have advanced technological knowledge and the wisdom to encode it in viral stories having symbols which humans would naturally and faithfully propagate through time. Perhaps the teachers were hoping their encoded knowledge would one day help us to advance our species when we became consciously aware of the deeper levels of encoded meaning.

Putting together the layers of encoding in the papyrus hints at a deeper message: the Sun is alive, just as cells are; as above, so below.

Rupert Sheldrake, English scientist and author, has this to say on the subject:

I think much good will come from recovering a sense of the life of the heavens. We are coming to see the Earth, Gaia, as alive. I think we also have to take seriously the idea that the Sun is alive and conscious. If one wants a scientific rationale for this, it comes ready to hand through the discoveries of modern solar physics. We now know that the Sun has a complex system of magnetic fields, reversing its polarity every eleven years, associated with the sunspot cycle. With this underlying rhythm of magnetic polar reversals are a whole series of resonant and harmonic patterns of magnetic and electromagnetic change - global patterns over the surface of the sun of a fractal nature; patterns within patterns, highly turbulent, chaotic, sensitive, varied and complex. As electromagnetic patterns within our brains seem to be the interface between the mind and the nervous system, here we have a parallel in the physical behavior of the sun. It is perfectly possible that the sun has a mind which interfaces with the solar system itself as an organism. This is largely what astrology has concerned itself with (see http://bit.ly/U6EaXr).

Chapter 4 - The Honeycomb and the Apple

The bee was the symbol of lower Egypt. The Pharaoh's title was "he of sedge and bee," meaning he (or occasionally she) was the ruler of upper and lower Egypt. Papyrus sedge is what ancient Egyptian writing material was made from.

The bee is required for pollination and without bees flowers do not transform into fruit. Aside from the agricultural practicality of keeping bees, these insects are potent symbols functioning on many levels.

The drones do the work collecting nectar and transforming it into honey for their queen and her young. This reality may have appealed to an elite who wished to live from the efforts of a worker class set below them in the social hierarchy.

Honey can be thought of as royal wisdom distilled from the nectar or knowledge collected by drones from flowers far and wide.

The beehive has long been a Masonic symbol and the hive is an emblem of the Lodge. Beehives are seen as a model of a just, orderly, industrious society and beehives are used as symbols on government buildings all over the world.

The executive wing of New Zealand's parliament building is called the Beehive because its shape is based on the traditional woven beehive, the skep, a hive made by beekeepers and used for over 2000 years. The building is 72m in height and the Queen Bee herself, Elizabeth II, officially opened it in 1977.

In antiquity, Mycenean tombs were shaped as beehives. The oracle priestess of Delphi was known as "the Delphic Bee." Priestesses worshipping Artemis were called Bees.

In Andrew Gough's fascinating research on bees, he wrote:

The Bee was a hugely important icon of Napoleon's reign, and his obsession with its symbolism led to his inevitable nickname; The Bee. Napoleon would have grown up with the symbolism of the Bee ingrained in his psyche, for his homeland of Corsica was required to pay the Romans an annual tax equivalent of £200,000 in Beeswax. The young emperor ensured that the Bee was widely adopted in his court as well as on clothing, draperies, carpets and furniture all across France. By choosing the Bee as the emblem of his reign, Napoleon was paying homage to Childeric (436 - 481), one of the 'long haired' Merovingian Kings of the region known as Gaul. When Childeric's tomb was uncovered in 1653, it was found to contain 300 golden jewels, styled in the image of a Bee. And of course, these are the same Bees that Napoleon had affixed to his coronation robe (see http://bit.ly/VP1kAU).

The following commemorative stone is located inside the Washington Monument at the 220-foot level. It reads, "Holiness to the Lord - Deseret" depicting a skep beehive under an all-seeing solar eye.

Deseret means "honeybee" and was proposed as the name of the western territory that later became the state of Utah, known today as the "Beehive State" with a state motto of "Industry."

According to most adherents of the Latter Day Saint movement, the Book of Mormon is a 19th century translation of a record inscribed on golden plates written by ancient inhabitants who lived on the American continent from approximately 2200 BC to 421 AD. -Wikipedia

In Chapter 9 of The Book of Mormon, verses 32 and 33 state the following:

32 And now, behold, we have written this record according to our knowledge, in the characters which are called among us the reformed Egyptian, being handed down and altered by us, according to our manner of speech.

33 And if our plates had been sufficiently large we should have written in Hebrew; but the Hebrew hath been altered by us also; and if we could have written in Hebrew, behold, ye would have had no imperfection in our record.

Interestingly Zion National Park is in the State of Utah. Its lowest elevation is 3666 feet, echoing the sidereal year of 366 days and the fact that the Earth is 366.6% the size of Moon.

Bees make a honeycomb to live in, raise their young, and store honey. Honeycomb has a hexagonal structure. Stacked logs form a hexagonal pattern, as do coins touching each other on a table. All snowflakes are hexagonal. Six most commonly makes its appearance within the non-living structure of the universe. The hexagon at the north pole of Saturn is case in point. As such 6 resonates with Osiris, Lord of the Dead.

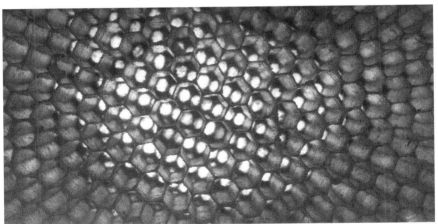

The apple is another potent symbol functioning on many levels. Eve became enlightened when she ate the forbidden fruit, and as a result was kicked out of paradise by a controlling immortal that didn't want humans to attain the awareness of gods.

The Forbidden Fruit by Michelangelo (1509)

The secret of the apple can be revealed to anyone who slices the fruit in half across its equator. Every apple conceals a pentagram, a secret in plain sight.

The pentagram inscribed in a circle was the symbol of the Pythagorean School. The upright pentagram is a symbol of magical protection, while the inverted pentagram is associated with black magic. Duality is present in all things.

The pentagram encodes Phi within itself as a fractal. The golden ratio proportions in the bodies of many life forms are beautifully illustrated in <u>The Power of Limits: Proportional Harmonies in Nature, Art & Architecture</u> by Gyorgy Doczi (Shambhala 1981).

5 is the number of nature and of living things. As such 5 resonates with Isis, goddess of nature.

Pierre-Simon Laplace (1749-1827) is remembered as one of the greatest scientists of all time. Encyclopaedia Britannica says, "Sometimes referred to as the Newton of France, Laplace possessed a phenomenal natural mathematical faculty, superior to that of any of his contemporaries."

Laplace noted (see http://bit.ly/Vmerxt) that ancient Mesopotamian calculations of the circumference of the Earth were based on a unit of 555 mm, which I will call the Laplace for lack of a better term.

If we consider the way the metric system was initially defined in Laplace's day, it was based on the assumption that the Earth measures exactly 40000 km in meridional circumference. There are exactly 72072072.072072... Laplaces in this measure. See Chapter 5 - Key Numbers for the significance of 72, 720 as well as 400.

If we instead accept the WGS84 value (the geodetic system that GPS satellites use) of 40007.86 km as the true meridional circumference of the Earth, I calculated that there are 72086400 Laplaces in this measure (99.9998%), thus encoding the number of god (72) and the number of the Sun (864) with a unit (555mm) which triply resonates with Isis, the goddess of nature. Either way you slice it 555 mm has an amazing resonance.

Relationships Between 6 and 5

Apples cannot exist without beehives to house the bees, which in turn pollinate the apple blossoms. Bees cannot exist without the nectar produced by the blossoms. We in turn cannot survive without bees doing their jobs, pollinating our agricultural products. Life is interrelated with the structures that support it. There is no part of the Earth untouched by life. Even the oldest sediments on this planet have been transformed by the earliest life forms.

The relationship between honeycomb and apple, between structure and life, is a sacred marriage.

The ancient Egyptians encoded this relationship in the Bent Pyramid of Dahshur, which was contemporaneous with the Great Pyramid of Giza. The Bent Pyramid has two slopes whose precise angles unfold into pentagons and hexagons, as animated in Secrets In Plain Sight - Volume 1 in the Egypt Part 2 episode.

The color of sunlight is standardized by black-body radiation having a temperature 6500 degrees above absolute zero (degrees Kelvin). This is another play of 6 and 5 with the scalar decimal value of 1,000.

The relationship between Phi and Pi is as follows:

$Pi / Phi^2 = 6/5$

This equation is extremely accurate (99.998%) but isn't exact. As such mathematicians classify it as recreational math, and don't take it seriously. They are missing a key relationship, as it is provably impossible to form an exact ratio between transcendental Pi and irrational Phi. Nevertheless this approximation relating Pi to Phi squared with the 6/5 ratio has astonishing accuracy.

Both Phi and Pi are encoded in the proportions of the cross section of the Great Pyramid. If the height of the pyramid is 4 then half its base length is Pi. On the other hand if the half-base is 1 then the length of the face of the pyramid (the hypotenuse of the triangle) is Phi.

Giza is 6.5 degrees north of the Tropic of Cancer, the line marking the most northerly latitude where the Sun appears directly overhead at its zenith.

Earth's polar circumference = 6/5 x 33,333,333 meters (99.98%).

Earth's mean circumference = 6/5 x 12^4 miles (99.99%).

*****

Paris was named after an ancient temple of Isis (see Chapter 1) and therefore resonates with 5, which geometrically speaking is a pentagon. France is colloquially known as *l'hexagone* because its shape on a map has long been recognized as a hexagon. I made the following piece of art illustrating the relationship between France and the location of her capital Paris (marked by the bee in the pentagon) using the illustration of the goddess Liberty from the logo of the current French Republic.

I'm not the first to perceive the importance of relating 6 to 5. Athanasius Kircher is best known for his <u>Oedipus Aegyptiacus</u> (1652-54), a vast syncretic study of alchemy, astrology, Kabbala, Pythagorean math, Greek myth, and a comparative study of languages. In it he incorporated information from Tito Burattini who measured the Great Pyramid with John Greaves as mentioned in Chapter 2.

Here is a detail from Kircher's amazing frontispiece from <u>Arithmologia</u> (1665) which in its entirety features a nine pointed star, the magic square of Saturn, the Ptolemaic ordering of the planets, a 3-4-5 triangle, the numbers 1,2,3,4 from the Pythagorean tetractys, and cherubs holding banners reading 'measures', 'weights', and 'number' (see frontispiece http://bit.ly/O98iN4). To me this reveals Kircher was trying to decipher the same code I am. There is a structure to reality and all these subjects are paths into the mystery.

Take a look at what is open on the awestruck man's lap: a book with a hexagram on his left and a pentagram on his right.

The Great Fire of 1666 happened the year after <u>Arithmologia</u> was published. On September 11th of that year Sir Christopher Wren proposed a new plan for London, which secretly encoded the triple-columned Kabbalistic Tree of Life that Kircher himself had published.

Wren's city plan wasn't adopted due to practical reasons but Charles II did commission Wren to redesign St. Paul's cathedral. St. Paul's cathedral is 6666 inches long including its entrance steps. From ground level to the top of the Cathedral's cross is 365 feet, resonating with the solar year. It's location coincides with the Sephira of the Sun in the Tree of Life encoded in Wren's 9/11/1666 plan of London.

Another structure using the amazing connection between feet and inches...

6666 inches = 555.5 feet

...is the Washington Monument in DC. Its official height is 555' 5-1/8", so it is just 3/8" shy of the ideal measurement of 555' 5.5" - very impressive for the world's largest masonry obelisk. Its sides are one tenth this dimension at 55.5 feet.

The front of the Great Seal of the United States features a Eagle with 33 feathers on one wing and 32 on the other. 3+3=6 and 3+2=5. Also 33+32=65. The feathers come together in a kind of number alchemy, transmuting into relationships between 6 and 5.

The word alchemy comes from *al-kemi* meaning "from Khem" or "from the black land" referring to the Nile delta. Isaac Newton, who is considered to be one of the most influential scientists to ever live, was foremost an alchemist. Western scientists transmuted alchemy into chemistry, a word which shares the same root.

Consider the following molecules which all are hexagons bonded to pentagons (indoles). These chemicals are all created in the human brain.

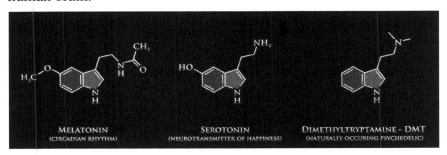

MELATONIN
(CIRCADIAN RHYTHM)

SEROTONIN
(NEUROTRANSMITTER OF HAPPINESS)

DIMETHYLTRYPTAMINE - DMT
(NATURALLY OCCURING PSYCHEDELIC)

Melatonin controls our circadian rhythm with the Sun. Serotonin makes us feel happy.

Sunshine on my shoulders makes me happy....sunshine almost always makes me high. -John Denver

DMT allows consciousness to leave the physical body and explore the universe. See <u>DMT The Spirit Molecule</u> (Inner Traditions 2001) by Rick Strassman, M.D.

The first scientists also transmuted astrology into astronomy. On 8/8/11 NASA-funded astronomers announced the discovery of adenine and guanine nucleobases, which are components of DNA, found in 12 meteorites (one for each sign of the zodiac).

The team is confident these compounds were generated in space inside asteroids or comets (see http://1.usa.gov/ojQC0m). Look at the molecular structures they discovered: hexagons bonded to pentagons, the precursors of life inside a rock.

Image by NASA's Goddard Space Flight Center / Chris Smith

If meteorites hitting Earth have DNA nucleobases in them, then this suggests life is seeded everywhere by meteorites. This discovery validates the ancient Greek idea of *panspermia*. In other words, we know that life exists everywhere on Earth that it possibly can, even in hot hydrothermal vents under the ocean, in acid, in salt, in bitter cold, under high pressure, and in many other extreme environments. Logically, if life exists everywhere that it possibly can exist (within certain environmental limits of course), and meteorites essentially seed life, then we are certainly not alone in the galaxy.

A galaxy is composed of gas and dust and stars - billions upon billions of stars. -Carl Sagan in the TV series Cosmos (1980)

I will close this chapter with piece of art I made called "Transcendence" which encodes many instructive symbols. I will elaborate my take on the encoded symbolism. The piece is built on the proportions of a 33-56-65 Pythagorean triangle.

33 x 33 + 56 x 56 = 65 x 65

In this triangle we have the key number 33 entangled with mirror versions of the 6-5 relationship in 56 and 65.

"Transcendence" by Scott Onstott

The human spinal column of 33 vertebrae represents what 33 is all about: the full journey up Jacob's ladder.

The molecule depicted is DMT; a prime example of the alchemy the human brain is capable of performing. It represents our innate potential to transmute the mundane dross we consume as food into the chemicals of ecstasy and spiritual transcendence, from the amino acid tryptophan to the spirit molecule dimethyltryptamine.

The 5x5 magic square is associated with Mars because of its position as the fifth sephira Gevurah in the Kabbalistic Tree of Life, which is associated with Mars (see Lesson 6 in the Esoteric Astronomy episode in Secrets In Plain Sight - Volume 1). The sum of every row, column, and diagonal in the Mars magic square adds up to 65.

The circle inside the triangle has a diameter of 24 exactly. The clock marks the hours as the Earth rotates through its 24 hour cycle, the yin and yang symbol within recalling AM and PM or day and night. The hands point at intersection points in the squaring the circle diagram, indicating the clockmakers' encoded time 10:08. The circle inside the triangle is about the Sun, Moon, and time, implying many of the cycles and cosmic harmonies discussed previously.

The human at the center of the clock sits contemplating the universe, and through his pineal gland at the center of the brain, his consciousness remotely views Mars, perhaps searching for evidence of life.

Chapter 5 - Key Numbers

There are certain key numbers above 9 around which disparate fundamental phenomena converge. The fact that this happens at all suggests a deep structuring of reality in number. These key numbers bear the signature of order rather than randomness. Order is a characteristic we have always perceived in Nature and which many have reasonably associated with conscious intentionality. Are we living in a computer simulation, a numerical matrix of sorts? Are we inside the mind of God? Are we ourselves active if sometimes unwitting participants in the design? Are extra-terrestrials, fourth-dimensional beings, or the gods themselves responsible? Contemplating the key numbers leads to deep philosophical questions about the nature of reality. In some way we close a grand circuit by becoming aware of the key numbers and what they encode. In this light I present 9 key numbers for your consideration.

Twenty Four

The mean solar day has exactly 24 hours. We have been measuring time this way for as long as we have kept written records or passed tradition down orally.

Gold, the coveted metal, which has always been associated with the Sun, is assigned a purity of 24 carats when it is 99.9% gold or higher.

In Chapter 3 - Measuring Time I presented research that our solar system is in a larger binary system with the Sirius system. Cruttenden's Binary Companion Theory elegantly explains the phenomenon of Earth's precession. This long cycle, known as the Great Year, has been calculated having a period of 24,000 years.

In Chapter 1 - The Decimal System and the Ennead I presented the case for the decimal system as a powerful encoder of the laws from which physical reality is constructed. The zeros are placeholders in the decimal system indicating a scaling factor or transformation that does not alter number quality. Therefore the number 24,000 has the same quality as 24.

The orbit our system experiences relative to the Sirius system is elliptical and because of the physics of this geometry, the rate of precession changes over time. In recent times the earth has been precessing at its minimum rate of change of 1 degree every 72 years and the Great Year was extrapolated from this minimum rate as 72 x 360 = 25,920 years. The average rate of precession is 66.66 years which gives a new value for the Great Year of 66.66 x 360 = 24,000.

The traditional figure for the Great Year of 25,920 Earth years can be decomposed into 24 x 1080. 24 is associated with the solar day, and the lunar radius is 1080 miles (99.9%).

Drawing by Albrect Durer from his Nuremberg Chronicle (1493)

Leonardo Fibonacci of Pisa's <u>Liber Abaci</u> (1202) not only introduced the Indian zero, Arabic numerals (1-9), and the decimal place system to the West, but this brilliant Italian mathematician is also credited with a famous sequence bearing his name.

The Fibonacci sequence starts with nothing (0) and then moves to something (1). There is one simple rule to construct the rest of the sequence: *each number is the sum of the previous two numbers.* The Fibonacci sequence therefore begins

0,1,1,2,3,5,8,13,21,34,55,89,144,...

An interesting property of this sequence is that successive adjacent terms in the sequence form ratios approximating Phi. Each ratio is alternately above and then below the golden number, getting ever closer as the sequence progresses.

$$89/55 \quad = \quad 1.618181818$$
$$144/89 \quad = \quad 1.617977528$$
$$233/144 \quad = \quad 1.618055556$$
$$377/233 \quad = \quad 1.618025751$$
$$610/377 \quad = \quad 1.618037135$$
$$987/610 \quad = \quad 1.618032787$$
$$\Phi \quad = \quad 1.618033989$$

Another property is that you can start the Fibonacci sequence with any two numbers. The successive terms will still approximate Phi. The golden number is encoded within recursion itself.

If instead of taking ratios of terms you reduce the Fibonacci sequence to its digital roots, a cyclical pattern emerges. The Fibonacci sequence's digital roots repeat with a period of 24.

The following is an illustration I made revealing this cycle. Starting with 1, the digital root to the right of top-dead-center, and then moving clockwise we have 1,2,3,5,8, and then 4 because the digital root of 13 is 4. The next term is 3 because it is the digital root of 21 in the Fibonacci sequence, and so on. The digital roots repeat in this pattern as the cycle continues moving clockwise around the circle.

"Spiral of Life" by Scott Onstott

Notice that all opposite digital roots across the diameter of the circle have 9 as their digital roots. The number 9 is a symbol of completeness, expressed in idioms such as *the whole nine yards, a cat has nine lives,* and *she was on cloud nine.* A human baby grows for 9 months before being born. The repetition of nines suggests a kind of internal wholeness, as .999999999... is essentially one.

*****

Peter Plichta discovered what he called the Prime Number Cross in God's Secret Formula: Deciphering the Riddle of the Universe and the Prime Number Code, a book that I mentioned in Chapter 1. Plichta recognized that all prime numbers follow a pattern that is recognizable when you array all numbers around a circle having 24 divisions or rays. The only exceptions are the numbers 2 and 3, which are in the initial trinity of numbers.

Here is my illustration of this concept:

"Meditation on 24" by Scott Onstott

The prime numbers become less and less frequent the further out you go from the center in a way that is bound to **e**, a transcendental number like Pi that I'll discuss in Chapter 6.

Plichta developed a four-dimensional theory of atomic structure based on the prime number space depicted above with 24 rays emanating from the nucleus, like rays of the Sun.

I placed a ring of Egyptian uni-literals around the ring because the ancient 24-letter alphabet resonates with the hours of the day, the rays of the Sun, the 24 digital roots of the Fibonacci sequence, the pattern within prime numbers, and the 4D structure of the atom.

24 is a number that resonates with cyclic order in Nature and Reality.

Thirty Three

33 is the number of the journey from beginning to end, the full range, the entire reign, a coming of age, the alpha to the omega. Consider the following correlations:

Scottish Rite freemasons hold 33 as their highest degree. 33 is entangled with 32. The 32nd degree is the highest degree an initiate can earn. Only those selected by the 33rd degree holders on the supreme council can become fellow 33rd degree members. In this way 33 is associated with the final goal of the secret tradition.

The Kabbalistic Tree of Life has 10 sephiroth and 22 paths between them, which adds to 32 elements. The hidden sephira Da'at, which represents the mystical state where all 10 sephiroth are united as one, brings the sum total of elements up to the magic 33.

The eagle on the Great Seal of the United States correlates with the Scottish Rite in having 33 feathers on one wing and 32 on the other.

Immediately after being sworn in, the President of the United States of America ascends 33 steps into the Capitol Rotunda. Thanks to investigative mythologist William Henry for this connection. Henry writes, "It is crystal clear that the builders viewed the Capitol as America's sole temple (a solemn, Solomon's Solar Temple to be exact)." See http://bit.ly/OFN4fr

King David, father of Solomon, reigned in Jerusalem for 33 years.

In the Holy Bible, Numbers Chapter 33 details all the stages of the Israelites journey out of Egypt, a tale told in 56 verses.

Call unto me, and I will answer thee, and show thee great and mighty things, which thou knowest not. -Jeremiah 33:3

Jesus was crucified at age 33 and is said to have performed 33 miracles.

The Dome of the Rock is 33 miles from the sea.

The Muslim lunar calendar gets synchronized with the solar year every 33 Muslim years.

The northernmost tip of Israel, Mount Zion or Baal-Hermon as it is also known, is at a latitude of 33 degrees. The highest permanently manned United Nations outpost is on the summit of Mt. Zion.

The United Nations emblem divides the world into 33 sectors.

Greater London is divided into 32 boroughs. The City of London is the 33rd jurisdiction, an independent city within the metropolis. The London Eye has 32 cars revolving around its central pivot or eye. It appears to be held up by Masonic compasses.

It takes light 3.3 nanoseconds to travel one meter.

The Sun is 333,000 times more massive than the Earth.

Earth's polar circumference is 6/5 x 33,333,333 meters (99.98%).

The largest gold repository in the world is located at 33 Liberty Street in New York City.

The volume of the Sun is 33 orders of magnitude larger than a marble.

The "shortest measurable length" in the universe, called the Plank length, is 33 orders of magnitude smaller than a marble.

Middle C, the middle point of the range in which humans perceive sound, is 33 harmonics above the Schumann resonance, the fundamental vibration of the Earth.

The human spinal column has 33 vertebrae.

The pressure of the Earth's atmosphere is equivalent to a column of water 33 feet high. Every 33 feet you descend below the surface of Earth's oceans, the pressure increases by 1 atmosphere.

Escape velocity, or the speed one must exceed to leave Earth, is 33 times the speed of sound, known as Mach 33 (11.1 km/sec).

At Kennedy Space Center, where all Apollo and Space Shuttle missions left Earth, is NASA's Runway 33. It parallels the coast's angle of 330 degrees true north.

Spaceport America, where Virgin Galactic's space planes leave Earth, is located exactly on the 33rd parallel out in the middle of nowhere, New Mexico.

It's not far from Spaceport America to Launch Complex 33 (also all by itself in the middle of the New Mexico desert) where Werner Von Braun inaugurated America's space program with the remaining German V2 rockets left over from WW2, rockets that he developed to bomb London. Former SS Sturmbannführer Von Braun later designed the 33.0 foot diameter Saturn V rocket, which remains the tallest, heaviest, and most powerful rocket ever made.

Stonehenge is 33.33 degrees distant from the Dome of the Rock. Stonehenge's largest circle of standing stones measures 33 meters (108 ft) in diameter. The average distance between standing stones is 1.0 meter (3'3") and the average width of the lintels on top of the standing stones is 1.0 meter (3'3").

33 embodies the journey of the soul from initiation to enlightenment.

Thirty Six

Heinrich Cornelius Agrippa defined the magic square of the Sun in De Occulta Philosophia (circa 1510) as a 6x6 grid of 36 numbers whose every column and row adds up to 111. The sum of all the columns or rows is 666.

The term *Shemhamphorasch* refers to both the 216 (216 = 6 x 6 x 6) letter name of God in the Kabbalah (arranged in 72 word-triplets) and the *tetragrammaton*, or 4 letter name of God which is so holy it must never be pronounced.

The sum of the numbers 1 through 36 is 666. Thus, 36 has an occult resonance with the Sun and God.

Incidentally, the number of the Moon divided by the occult number of the Sun approximates Phi, namely 1080/666 = Phi (99.8%).

360 degrees is a full circle. The circle has always been a symbol of

femininity, and thus 36 resonates also with the Moon.

Sirius, the star of Isis, is the leader of the 36 decan constellations depicted in the Dendera Zodiac, now in the Louvre. There are 36 decans in the ancient Egyptian 360 day calendar.

The French Revolutionary calendar had 36 decades (10 day weeks) plus 5 or 6 intercalary days to synch with the solar year.

The central point of the Cergy-Pontoise complex northwest of Paris, is the square Belvedere Tower designed by architect Ricardo Bofill in 1986. The long straight phallic tower is 36m high, with sides one-tenth this dimension at 3.6 meters long. The tower is at the center of a ring of 360 paving stones (symbolizing the feminine) measuring 36 centimeters each. The tower with its surrounding circle forms a circumpunct, or point within a circle, which is a traditional solar symbol.

The Belvedere tower sits at the meeting point of the major and minor axes of the complex, surrounded by a semicircle of buildings, perhaps symbolizing the Sun's arcing path through the dome of the sky. A 3.6 meter wide path cuts a 3.6 meter opening through the semicircle and continues along the major axis. I have much more to say about this complex in Chapter 8 - Encoded Architecture and Cities.

J.K. Rowling's <u>Harry Potter and the Philosopher's Stone</u> (Raincoast Books 2000), the first installment of the best-selling book-series in history, has a connection to the modern Cergy-Pontoise because the medieval village Pontoise was the birthplace of Nicolas Flamel, the alchemist who in the 14th century made the philosopher's stone and from it supposedly attained eternal life.

Rowling's "he who must not be named" character Voldemort reminds me of the tetragrammaton, another powerful being whose name must not be pronounced.

In Chapter 13, Hermione pulls out a book she "got from the library weeks ago for some *light* reading" [emphasis my own] to discover that Nicolas Flamel was the creator of the philosopher's stone. Sharp Hermione also discovered that, "Flamel celebrated his six hundred and sixty-fifth birthday last year." In Rowling's story, Flamel lives 666 years before he chooses to die. 36 and 666 are alchemically entangled in Cergy-Pontoise.

The number of prime numbers up to 36 is 11. 11 x 11 is the number of prime numbers up to 666.

The ancient Sumerian long cycle, called a Shar, is exactly 3600 years. Fans of the late Zecharia Sitchin and his Earth Chronicles series of books, published from 1976-2007, know that he claimed the Shar measures the orbital period of the cataclysm-bringer Nibiru, which is the name of the disruptive planet that Sitchin says orbits our Sun out of the plane of the ecliptic.

The number of degrees in all the angles of an icosahedron is 3600.

The internal angle of every regular pentagram is 36 degrees. This angle is the key to much wisdom that you will learn about in Chapter 6 - Number Patterns.

One Hundred Fifty Three

The number 153 is the sum of the first 5 factorials: 1! + 2! + 3! + 4! + 5! where the exclamation point means the product of all integers less than or equal to the number. For example 5! = 5 x 4 x 3 x 2 x 1.

The curvy *vesica piscis*, a name that means "vessel of the fish," is a feminine symbol. Straight lines drawn inside it forming a rhombus shape symbolize the masculine. The Christian fish and the Pisces astrological symbols come from the vesica piscis.

If the width of a vesica piscis is 1 then its height would be exactly equal to the irrational square root of 3.

Rationally speaking, if the width is instead set equal to 153, then the height would be 265 as 265/153 is an excellent approximation of the square root of 3 (99.99%).

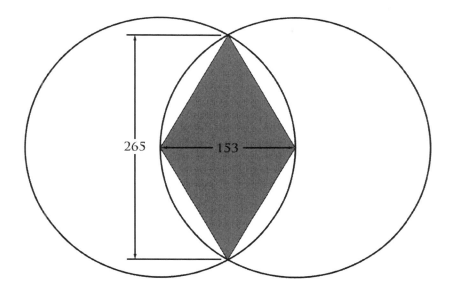

The following mysterious passage has puzzled biblical scholars for centuries:

Simon Peter went up, and drew the net to land full of great fishes, a hundred and fifty and three: and for all there were so many, yet was not the net broken. -John 21:11

Why count the fish? The number is arguably a code about structure of the unbreakable net we are all caught in: reality.

The Tetragrammaton occurs 153 times in the Book of Genesis, another reference to this mysterious code.

The ancient Egyptian obelisk in St. Peter's Square is another solar phallic symbol. Jan Thulstrup counted 153 statues atop St. Peter's Square in the Vatican. Why 153? I think the root cause is because the square root of 153 is the number of lunar months in a year (99.99%). When you understand the symbolism, Bernini's enclosure in St. Peter's Square becomes a womb enclosing the son.

Sun and Moon are thus encoded in the Catholic axis mundi.

James Furia says that 360 feet up the Great Pyramid is the 153rd course of masonry and the Grand Gallery within the Great Pyramid is 153 feet long. He also shows the following:

153 x Pi = Height of the Great Pyramid in feet (99.9%)
153 / Pi = Inner radius of Stonehenge's sarsen ring in feet (97%)

In <u>Pyramidology</u> (1970), Adam Rutherford noted that there are 153 courses of masonry from the top of the Great Pyramid to the floor of the King's chamber.

I noticed that the niche in the Queen's chamber is 15.3 feet high.

Another great pyramid in Paris encodes 153 and entangles it with 36 and 666, as shown in Secrets In Plain Sight - Volume 1. The Louvre Pyramid's glass is divided into 153 rhombic panes on each face. Each of the larger rhombic frames contains 36 rhombic panes of glass.

Tabulating the additional small glass triangles, converting them to rhombi (2 equilateral triangles = 1 rhombus), and then adding the number of larger rhombic frames we get 166.5 symbolic rhombi in a typical face. Four such faces (166.5 x 4) equals 666.

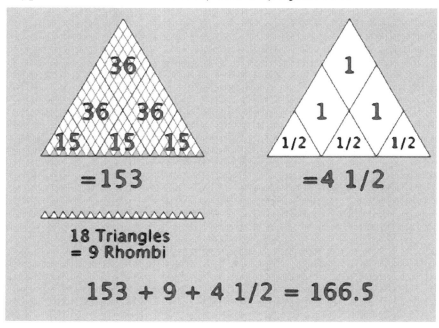

Both 666 and 153 are triangular numbers. In addition the numbers 1,5, and 3 relate in a curious way:

$153 + 513 = 666; 135 + 531 = 666; 315 + 351 = 666$

In Secrets In Plain Sight Volume 2, I showed how squaring the circle actually encodes a Great Pyramid slope angle of 51.76 degrees.

The azimuth of summer solstice sunrise on the Louvre Pyramid is 51.76 degrees true north. The Louvre pyramid thus encodes Sun and Moon and acts like a shining hologram reflecting the Great Pyramid in the city of Isis.

There are 153 stanzas in the book The Hidden Words (1857), which was written by Bahaullah, the founder of the Baha'i Faith. The founder's son said that book is "a treasury of divine mysteries" and that when one ponders its contents, "the doors of the mysteries will open."

153 is a lunar doorway reflecting the mysteries, just as the Moon reflects the Sun.

Two Hundred Seventy Three

Imagine a circle inscribed precisely within a square. The square has 27.3% more area than the circle.

Now imagine a circle and a square having the same perimeter (this is called squaring the circle by length). The circle's diameter is 27.3% longer than any edge of the square.

The amazing thing is, the Moon is 27.3% the size of the Earth.

How could the Earth-Moon system be expressed more simply and elegantly than by this pure geometric relationship between a circle and a square? Great truths are this simple. Reality bears the signature of design and this necessarily implies consciousness. However I am not saying that consciousness is God, and will leave that to you to contemplate.

A circle is an infinite number of points on a plane equidistant from a center. The circle gives boundary to the infinite, a womb to the creation, a shape to the Moon and Sun discs. A square has four equal straight sides and four right angles. As the four cardinal directions arise from the square (or possibly the other way around), finite orthogonal property boundaries can be surveyed in the landscape, and civilization and temple building can proceed in an orderly way. With a square the irrational can be rationalized, brought down to Earth, and made practical.

The Moon's sidereal rotation period is 27.3 days. That's the time it takes the moon to complete one revolution around the Earth relative to the fixed stars. Human menstrual periods on the other hand tend to resonate with the Moon's synodic period of 29.5 days, the lunar month.

However, human gestation lasts on average 273 days showing a resonance with 10 times the sidereal or star period of the Moon. Water becomes liquid 273 degrees above absolute zero. Our bodies are made mostly of water. We are holographic expressions of cosmic cycles.

The sidereal solar year of 366 days (as discussed in Chapter 3) is mathematically linked to 273 through two uncanny ratios:

$1/27.3 = .0366$
$1/366 = .00273$

The rational message is: the Moon's rotation about the Earth in some way reflects the Earth's rotation about the Sun, both relative to the fixed stars.

273 is a number that harmonizes with the cosmos; as above, so below.

Four Hundred

400 is another number that resonates with Sun, Moon, and Earth.

The great circle running through Earth's north and south poles was initially defined in 1793 as having a circumference of exactly 40,000 kilometers, thus grounding the metric system in the Earth. As measurements have become more precise, we know that this relationship is 99.98% accurate as the Earth's actual meridional circumference is slightly larger at 40,007.86 km.

Irrespective of units of measure, the following proportions relate Sun, Moon, and Earth:

The Sun is 400 times larger than the Moon (99.8%)

The Sun is an average of 400 times farther from the Earth than the Moon (97%)

These relationships encode something truly miraculous, the phenomenon of a total solar eclipse. This happens when the lunar disc perfectly covers the solar disc as seen from Earth and can only be viewed from within the shadow's umbra which is approximately 100 km wide on the Earth's surface. Within the umbra solar flares and the Sun's corona are all that extend beyond the surface of the Sun.

This is an actual photo of the perfection of the total solar eclipse of 1999:

Image credit Luc Viatour/lucnix.be under the Creative Commons BY-SA 3.0 license.

The size of the lunar disc varies over the course of a lunar month due to *libration*, the oscillating motion of the orbit of the Moon relative to the orbit of the Earth. It is remarkable that the size of the lunar disc only matches the solar disc perfectly at a new moon, which is the only time a total solar eclipse can occur.

The Moon's orbit is getting larger at a rate of 3.8 cm/year. In the distant future a total solar eclipse will no longer be possible, yet right now the relationship is perfect.

If the Moon was smaller and orbited closer to the Earth there would be another possible lunar orbital distance (or conversely if it was larger and farther away) where a total solar eclipse could happen. However the proportions relating Moon, Sun, and Earth would no longer converge on the number 400.

Is this just a happy accident against astronomical odds or is some deep intelligence coordinating all this? There is nothing in physics as I understand it that causes the Moon to be just the right size and just the right distance from the Earth, and the Earth just the right distance from the Sun to cause the resonance with the number 400. Another coincidence is that fact that the Earth's 40 million meter meridional circumference resonates with this same number quality, 4.

Four Hundred Thirty Two

The Sun's radius is 432,000 miles (99.8%).

432 x 432 is the speed of light in miles per second (99.8%)

In Chapter 3 - Measuring Time under the section "Sirius Does Not Precess", I presented research on why there are two figures for the Earth's precessional period, 25,920 and 24,000 years, representing the maximum projected rate versus the average rate under Cruttenden's Binary Companion Theory. The following equations show the relationship of 432 to the Great Year:

432 x 60 = 25920 years
432 x 55.555... = 24,000 years.

It has been said that the original Stradivarius violin was designed to be tuned to A = 432 cycles per second (Hertz).

There is a movement to change concert tuning to A = 432 Hz because it resonates better with the human voice and sounds more natural (see http://bit.ly/PxtOQj). Giuseppe Verdi, one of the most influential composers of operas of all time, believed that "432 Hz must be the A for opera."

If one tunes A = 432 Hz then the following frequencies result by dividing each note by the twelfth root of 2, using the twelve-tone equal temperament tuning system used today:

Note	Octave 1	Octave 2	Octave 3
A	**432**	**216**	**108**
G#	408	204	102
G	385	192	96
F	363	182	91
F#	343	171	86
E	324	**162**	**81**
D#	305	**153**	76
D	288	144	**72**
C#	**272**	136	68
C	257	128	64
B	242	121	61
A#	229	114	57

The mathematical constant e is 2.72, 6x6x6=216, Phi is 1.62, the key numbers 153, 108, 81, and 72 all resonate under 432 Hz tuning.

Note that standard concert pitch today is not A = 432 Hz but A = 440 Hz. At 440 Hz, all the frequencies in the above chart are shifted and thus do not resonate with the aforementioned numbers.

He who knows the secret of sound, knows the mystery of the whole universe. -Hazrat Inayat Khan

432 is also part of a key halving/doubling sequence: 108, 216, 432, 864, 1728, 3456. So 108 is in an important sequence with 432. 108 is a cosmic number harmonizing the following relationships:

Venus is an average of 108 million km from the Sun, (99.8%)
The Sun's diameter is approximately 108 Earth diameters (99%)
The Earth is 108 solar diameters from the Sun, (99.5%)
The Moon is 108 lunar diameters from the Earth, (98%)
The Moon's radius is 1080 miles (99.9%).

The element silver, which has always been associated with the Moon, has an atomic weight of 108.

Aside from the cosmic symbolism, 108 is also present in popular culture without most people being aware of it.

There are 108 stitches on a baseball. The highest frequency in FM radio is 108 MHz. 108 is India's emergency telephone number akin to 911 in the United States.

Returning to our consideration of 432 itself, in <u>Fingerprints of the Gods</u> (Three Rivers Press 1996) Graham Hancock pointed out the following correlations:

The height of the Great Pyramid times 43,200 = Earth's polar radius in feet (99.7%)
The base perimeter times 43,200 = Earth's equatorial circumference in feet (99.4%).

At Borobudur in Indonesia, the largest Buddhist temple in the world, there are 432 Buddha statues placed in niches all around this manmade mountain of the Sun. On the top *Arupadhatu* level there are 72 stupas containing larger Buddha statues. 432 + 72 = 504. The radius of the Earth plus the radius of the Moon is 5040 miles (99.96%).

In the Hindu vedas, which are among the world's oldest sacred texts, the Kali yuga ("the age of vice") is said to last 432,000 years. Most interpreters of Hindu scriptures believe that Earth is currently in the Kali Yuga.

The word *veda* means "knowledge" in Sanskrit. The vedas are apauruseya ("not of human agency") and were supposedly directly revealed (sruti) rather than remembered (smrti).

It appears that knowledge of the numerical structure of reality was given to us by others, encoded into temples, but eventually almost completely forgotten. We are just now waking up from a long collective sleep and have started the process of remembering.

Five Hundred Twenty Eight

528 is a key number residing at the center of what has been termed the *solfeggio*, which includes the following numbers: 174, 285, 396, 417, 528, 639, 741, 852, 963.

I disagree with the popular idea that these so-called solfeggio numbers are musical frequencies mirroring the diatonic musical scale represented by the notes Do, Re, Mi, Fa, Sol, La, Ti (or the older Ut, Re, Mi, Fa, Sol, La). The spaces between the numbers do not fit musical intervals.

I do think these numbers are fundamentally important, but not as frequencies. To avoid confusion I will nonetheless call them the solfeggio numbers rather than introduce a new term.

The solfeggio numbers synchronize with the ennead in three equilateral triangles from which the numerals can be read in any order moving counterclockwise on each triangle.

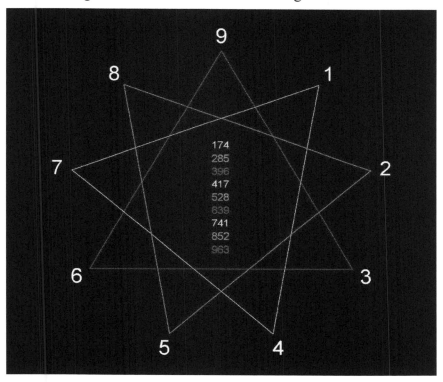

These three solfeggio triangles are analogous to astrological trine aspects (equilateral triangles within the 12 signs of the zodiac). Trines tend to indicate harmony, an ease of expression, or the source of innate artistic talent.

528 is the middle number of all the triangular aspects within the ennead, and perhaps that is what makes 528 such a key number.

There are exactly 5280 feet in a mile. One mile has exactly 63,360 inches because there are 12 inches in a foot. These numbers are entangled in the following relations:

Earth's mean circumference = $(6/5)^4$ x 63,360 x 1000 feet (99.99%)
Earth's mean circumference = $(6/5)$ x 12^4 miles (99.99%)
Earth's mean circumference = 24,883.2 miles (99.99%)
4D cubit = $(6/5)^4$ feet = 24.8832 inches exactly

1 inch / 1 mile = 1 astronomical unit / 1 light-year (99.9%) from Lawrence Edlund.

528 appears to be a harmonic structure of reality. If there were a different number of feet in a mile or a different number of inches in a foot none of this would harmonize so beautifully.

Seven Hundred Twenty

720 is a number symbolizing multiplicity itself, or a full complement of factors. 720 is a highly composite number having 30 divisors. One could say 720 has as many children as there are days in the month. 720 is also the number of degrees in two circles. In a geometric sense all the numerical progeny of 720 emerge from the intersection of the two circles of a vesica piscis.

The Sun and Moon discs each occupy approximately half a degree of arc as measured from the Earth. You would need 360 Suns plus 360 Moons (720 discs) to encompass the entire circle of the sky.

The number of degrees in all the angles of a tetrahedron is 720. The tetrahedron is the simplest 3D form.

720 has the same number quality as 72. There are 72 names of God in the Kabbalah.

The Librarian of Alexandria requested the high priest of Jerusalem select 6 men from each of the twelve tribes of Israel (6x12 = 72 interpreters) to come to Egypt and translate the Hebrew law into Greek.

The translators got to work in 72 chambers and finished their work in 72 days according to the second century BC "Letter of Aristeas." Their translation is called the Septuagint, which means 72.

The Christian Lord (and his angels?) confused human speech into 72 languages after they destroyed the Tower of Babylon.

And the Lord came down to see the city and the tower, which the children of men built. And the Lord said, Behold, the people is one, and they have all one language; and this they begin to do: and now nothing will be restrained from them, which they have imagined to do. Go to, let us go down, and there confound their language, that they may not understand one another's speech. -Genesis 11:5-7

Set's 72 disciples sealed Osiris in a coffin and sent it down the Nile.

Thoth won a 72nd part of the Sun's light from the Moon (360/72 = 5) in a game of chance and gave the sunlight to Nut, the goddess of the sky. Going against the wishes of the Sun god Ra, Nut got together with Geb, god of the Earth. Nut gave birth every day for 5 days to Set, Nephthys, Osiris, Isis, and Horus (within Isis). These 5 intercalary days rounded out the 365-day Sothic year.

The circle is a symbol of the entire horizon, giving a boundary to the infinite sky. The square is a symbol of a rationalized and ordered Earth. Geb and Nut coming together is analogous to squaring the circle.

One can never perfectly draw a square with the same perimeter as a circle because the circumference of any circle is Pi times its diameter. Pi is an infinite never repeating transcendental number that can never be perfectly rationalized and brought down to Earth.

However Pi and squaring the circle can be approximated in the real world and that is just what John Michell did in the City of Revelation (1973) when he discovered the key to a very precise squaring-the-circle diagram is a 3-4-5 triangle.

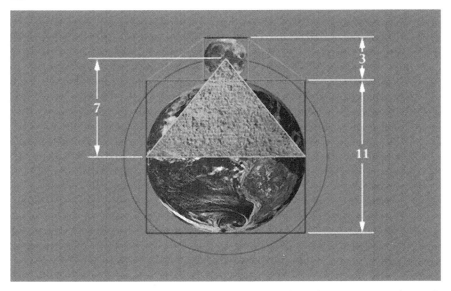

The incredible thing about this diagram is that the Moon and Earth actually fit its proportions with an accuracy of 99.97%. The diameter of the Moon compared to the diameter of the Earth has the proportions of 3:11. The proportions of the Great Pyramid (7:11) are also simultaneously encoded in this sacred geometry.

Michell also realized that if you scale the diagram **up by a factor of 720**, the diagram then encodes the true dimensions of the Moon and Earth in miles. The Moon's diameter is 2160 miles (99.94%) and the Earth's diameter is 7920 miles (99.97%). Michell called the following numbers *canonical*, suggesting they are the components of an ancient canon that humanity has been in the process of rediscovering in the last forty years:

1,080 miles, radius of Moon
2,160 miles, diameter of Moon
3,960 miles, radius of Earth
5,040 miles, combined radii of Moon and Earth
7,920 miles, diameter of Earth
10,080 miles, combined diameters of Moon and Earth

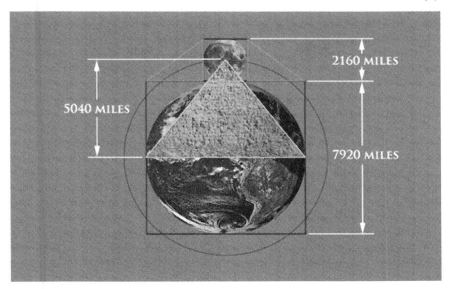

Michell shows that the distance from the Earth to the Moon is also encoded in the diagram. By inscribing a hexagon within the Earth circle in the above diagram and measuring its perimeter, he discovered that it is one-tenth the mean Moon-Earth distance (99.6%).

Perhaps the inscribed hexagon is hinted at by the fact that 720 = 6! or 6 x 5 x 4 x 3 x 2 x 1.

The Earth precesses one degree every 72 years in the traditional reckoning of the Great Year of 25,920 years. A month of the Great Year, called an Age, is 2160 years. As the famous song says "It is the dawning of the Age of Aquarius."

That which is Below corresponds to that which is Above, and that which is Above, corresponds to that which is Below, to accomplish the miracles of the One Thing. –The Emerald Tablet ascribed to Thoth (manuscript from 650 AD).

The temperature where humans are most comfortable is approximately 72 degrees Fahrenheit. For our bodies to remain at the biologically ideal internal temperature of 98.6 degrees we must continually dissipate excess heat to the environment. When the environment is at a temperature of 72 degrees, the heat flow off our skin is approximately balanced by the rate at which our cells generate internal heat (see http://bit.ly/WsjUVu).

The typical resting heart rate in adults is 62 - 82 beats per minute. At an average rate of 72 beats per minute, in 1 hour the heart will have beat 4320 times, resonating with the solar radius. In 12 hours the heart will have beat 51,840 times. The Great Pyramid slope is very close to 51.84 degrees.

Human sperm and ovum live approximately 72 hours.

We resonate with Sun, Moon, and Earth. Here is a visual correlation I made:

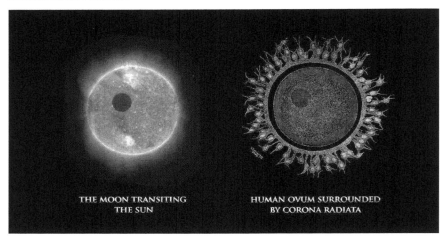

THE MOON TRANSITING
THE SUN

HUMAN OVUM SURROUNDED
BY CORONA RADIATA

More specifically, the macrocosmic view is from the STEREO-B spacecraft (2007) that, at some distance from the Earth, photographed our Moon transiting the Sun disc complete with solar corona. The human ovum in the microcosm on the right is from <u>Gray's Anatomy</u> depicting the corona radiata cells protecting the ovum before it is fertilized. The cell nucleus containing the mother's DNA is visible.

Chapter 6 - Number Patterns

Patterns emerge naturally from the study of numbers. By perceiving these patterns we gain insight and have the opportunity to expand our awareness deeper into the structures of reality.

Wherever there is number, there is beauty. -Proclus (5th century AD)

Sadly, many people's minds have been closed down to mathematics. This work does not require a strong background in math. Primarily we will appreciate beauty by exploring number patterns.

Number Categories

Mathematicians categorize numbers with labels such as *rational*, *irrational*, *transcendental*, and *imaginary*. Understanding these categories will help us to understand some of the patterns that exist within number. The illustration may help you to form a visual memory for these categories and their labels as we go on to explore them below.

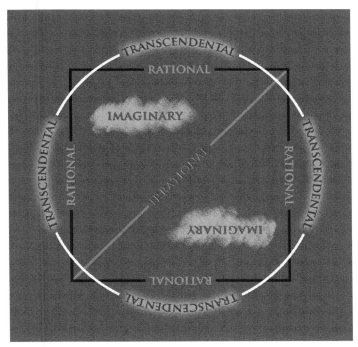

"Number Relationships" by Scott Onstott

Children learn to count with what are called natural numbers. At some point we learn how to form fractions from natural numbers like 132/25, and these ratios are called *rational* numbers (the word "rational" comes from "ratio").

When rational numbers are converted to decimals such as 132/25 = 5.28, the decimal expressions themselves are still considered rational numbers.

Some rational numbers form infinitely repeating decimals such as 1/9 = .111111... while other fractions repeat in longer patterns such as 1/7 = .142857142857... (the repeated pattern is 6 digits long in this case). However, not all infinite decimals repeat. For example consider a square. If you draw a square with an edge length of 1, its diagonal is the square root of 2 = 1.414213562... with digits going on infinitely, but without ever forming a repeating pattern.

Square roots apparently so traumatized Pythagoras that he is said to have thrown overboard a student who pointed out the fact that the length of the diagonal of a unit square cannot be expressed rationally, proven by the Pythagorean theorem itself!

Pythagoras' unacceptable behavior is echoed today in the term *irrational* which carries the connotation of being illogical or unreasonable.

Most people however probably think mathematicians went overboard with the invention of *imaginary* numbers. This happened because there is no rational or irrational number that can represent the square root of a negative number. This was solved by the invention of **i**. The letter **i** is used to denote the imaginary square root of negative 1. In other words, **i** squared equals negative 1, and by extension, 5**i** squared equals negative 25, so that **i** provides a way for mathematicians to express the square root of any negative number.

Paul Nahin gives the following account of the history of **i** in <u>An Imaginary Tale: The Story of the Square Root of Negative One</u> (Princeton University Press 1998):

In 1878, when two brothers stole a mathematical papyrus from the ancient Egyptian burial site in the Valley of the Kings, they led scholars to the earliest known occurrence of the square root of a negative number. The papyrus offered a specific numerical example of how to calculate the volume of a truncated square pyramid, which implied the need for **i**.

In the first century AD, the mathematician-engineer Heron of Alexandria encountered **i** *in a separate project, but fudged the arithmetic; medieval mathematicians stumbled upon the concept while grappling with the meaning of negative numbers, but dismissed their square roots as nonsense.*

By the time of Descartes, a theoretical use for these elusive square roots - now called imaginary numbers - was suspected, but efforts to solve them led to intense, bitter debates. The notorious **i** *finally won acceptance and was put to use in complex analysis and theoretical physics in Napoleonic times.*

I find it especially interesting that the calculation of the volume of the Great Pyramid implied the need for the imaginary **i**.

The golden number Phi is considered to be an irrational (but real) number because it can be expressed algebraically with a square root. Phi is one-half plus the square root of 5 divided by two, which equals 1.618033988749895...

A simple 2 to 1 rectangle, or double square, encodes both Phi and Pi. The King's chamber in the Great Pyramid has the proportions of 1 on the long edge to 1/2 on the short edge (or 2 to 1), like two squares placed adjacent to one another. If you draw a triangle with the long edge equal to 1 and the short edge 1/2, by the Pythagorean theorem its hypotenuse measures 1.118033988749895... (exactly one-half less than Phi).

You can also easily divide the 1 edge into perfect Phi proportions by pivoting a compass from opposite corners of the triangle as shown in the following diagram.

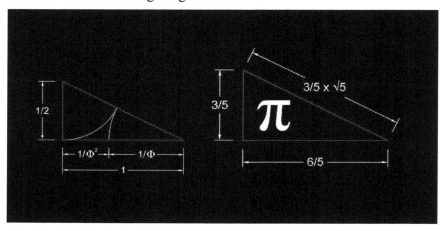

If you scale the triangle up by a factor of 6/5, its perimeter equals Pi (99.998%).

Pi is categorized as *transcendental*, meaning it is a number with infinite non-repeating decimals that cannot be represented algebraically with rational coefficients (something that is possible for irrational numbers). Pi is quite simply the relationship of a circle to its diameter, and this turns out to be a transcendental mystery of mathematics.

In 2011, Pi was calculated by Shigeru Kondo to 10 trillion places, a computation that took 44 terabytes of memory and more than a year to complete.

The mathematical constant **e** is another well-known transcendental number. **e** is fundamental in science as the base of the natural logarithm, which, among many other things, is used to calculate the distribution of prime numbers.

e is also fundamental in business. To understand this, imagine that you have an account with one hundred dollars that pays 100 percent interest. Fantastic! If the interest is credited once at the end of the year you will have $200. If the same interest is compounded every 6 months you will have $225. Compounding quarterly yields $244, and compounding monthly yields $261. With continuous compounding the account yields $271.83, which is **e** times 100.

When Google filed their initial public offering in 2004 the founders announced their intention to raise exactly **e** billion dollars or $2,718,281,828. The geeky and astute executives at Google must have understood that **e** represents the maximum return on investment. Just eight years later in 2012, Google has assets in excess of $72 billion, processes more than one billion search requests every day, and is the Internet's most visited website. It looks like invoking **e** worked out pretty well for Google.

e is 2.718281828... I noticed that **e** is suspiciously close to the megalithic yard.

By measuring more than 600 sites the Scottish engineer Alexander Thom defined the megalithic yard as 2.722 ±0.002 feet in A Statistical Examination of Megalithic Sites in Britain (1955).

Another interesting parallel is that the surface area of a sphere compared to the surface area of a tetrahedron inscribed within is Pi x Sqrt 3 / 2 which equals 2.7206...

In The Lost Science of Measuring the Earth John Michell and Robin Heath noted the following relationship:

Lunar month / (Solar year - Lunar year) = 29.53 days / (365.24 days - 354.37 days) = 2.72.

From this, John Michell and Robin Heath defined the *astronomical megalithic yard* as $(6/5)^3$ x 11/7 = 2.715428571428571... feet. Here again we have the 6/5 cubed relationship as discussed in Chapter 2 - Metrology. Notice also that 6/5 cubed is multiplied by the Great Pyramid's width to height proportion of 11/7, yielding the astronomical megalithic yard.

Interestingly, another way of exactly expressing the astronomical megalithic yard is 36/7 x .528 = 2.715428571428571... feet.

No matter which equation one uses to calculate the astronomical megalithic yard, it is approximately **e** feet (99.9%), which is between 32 and 33 inches in length, another amazing "coincidence."

Coincidence is God's way of remaining anonymous. -Albert Einstein

Euler's identity, which has been called "the most beautiful theorem in mathematics," relates **e**, **i**, Pi, unity, and the void.

It is $e^{Pi \times i} + 1 = 0$

Hugh Harleston had this to say about the pyramid complex in Teotihuacan Mexico:

Here was a design whose dimensional configurations provided accurate universal mathematical and other constants...laid out to incorporate the values of pi, phi, and e. Perhaps the pyramid complex was an intended hint to latecomers to expand their consciousness for a clearer view of the cosmos and of man's relation to the whole. -Re-quoted from <u>The Mars Mystery</u> *(Doubleday 1998) by Graham Hancock.*

I discovered, or perhaps rediscovered, the following relationship harmonizing Pi, Phi, e, and 528.

Phi / Pi = e / 5.28 (99.9%)

Sequences

Sequences of adjacent numbers are one of the keys to expanding one's awareness. For example, the *tetractys* was an important Pythagorean symbol in the school's reverence for number. The tetractys is composed of ten dots arranged in four rows with the sequence of 1,2,3, and 4 points in each row. Here is an ancient Pythagorean invocation:

Bless us, divine number, thou who generated gods and men! O holy, holy Tetractys, thou that containest the root and source of the eternally flowing creation! For the divine number begins with the profound, pure unity until it comes to the holy four; then it begets the mother of all, the all-comprising, all-bounding, the first-born, the never-swerving, the never-tiring holy ten, the keyholder of all. - quoted in <u>Number, the Language of Science</u> *by Tobias Dantzig (1930)*

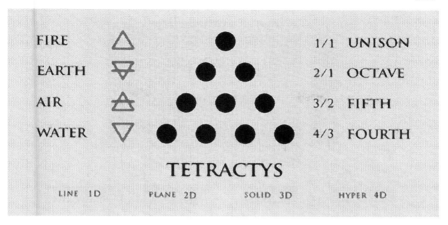

The tetractys encodes the four elements, the most harmonious just musical intervals, and represents the structure of four dimensions. Buckminster Fuller's *isotropic vector matrix* is a 3D equivalent of the tetractys. According to physicist Nassim Haramein, the isotropic vector matrix is at the core of the structure within the vacuum, supporting the emergence of physical reality from the underlying field. Haramein calculated that there is far more energy in the volume occupied by a marble than the energy output of all the Suns in the visible universe.

Space appears empty to us because it is perfectly balanced, but nothingness is anything but empty. The vacuum is a "seething cauldron of energy" in the words of physicist Tom Bearden. However because the energy is in a state of near-perfect balance it appears to us as if nothing is there in "space."

There is enough energy inside an empty coffee cup to evaporate all the world's oceans. -Richard Feynman, physicist

*****

Another example of an ordered sequence of numbers is 3456 ancient Egyptian royal miles in the Earth's polar radius (99.99%). A royal mile is defined as exactly 8/7 of a statute mile. Recall also that 3456 is the culmination of the following doubling sequence: 108, 216, 432, 864, 1728, 3456.

In The Lost Science of Measuring the Earth, Michell and Heath showed that there are 123.4 miles between the center of Lundy Island, and the center of Stonehenge in a heading running due east.

123.4 miles = 108 royal miles, another key number in the aforementioned doubling sequence. Lundy is the origin point of the greater temple that was discussed in Chapter 3, as well as in Secrets In Plain Sight - Volume 1.

The distance between the tallest prehistoric human-made mound in Europe (Silbury Hill) and the tallest modern building in the European Union (the Shard) is 123,456 meters, which is equivalent to 66.66 nautical miles.

66.66 = 33.33 + 33.33

33.33 x 33.33 = 1111 (99.99%)

1111 x 1111 = 1234321

If you multiply numbers together in a number line from 1 to 11 the following patterns emerge. This diagram is to be read as a multiplication number line. For example 1x2x3x4x5x6x7 = 7x8x9x10 = 5040.

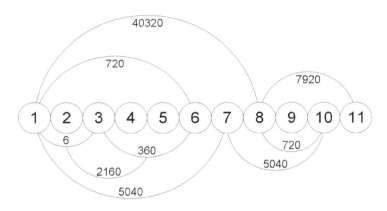

720 = 1x2x3x4x5x6 = 8x9x10
2160 = 6 x 360 = 6x6x6x10
2,160 miles, diameter of Moon
5,040 miles, combined radii of Moon and Earth = 7! = 7x8x9x10
7,920 miles, diameter of Earth = 8x9x10x11
40320 encodes the Sun's radius of 432,000 miles

Vedic Mathematics

In <u>The Language of Pattern: An Enquiry Inspired by Islamic Decoration</u> by Albarn, Smith, Steele, and Walker (Thames and Hudson 1974), the authors discuss the *Vedic Square* which they say, "...was the basis of a whole mathematical system which contained the numerical model of the universe. In AD 770 the Muslims integrated this North Indian system into their own synthesis of ancient systems."

The Vedic Square is composed of the digital roots of a child's multiplication table. I have labeled its rows and columns with letters to denote the patterns emerging from the sequences of digital roots. The prime patterns A'B'C'D' are in reverse sequence compared to the letter patterns ABCD. Pattern E stands alone as all 9's.

Child's Multiplication Chart

	1	2	3	4	5	6	7	8	9
1	1	2	3	4	5	6	7	8	9
2	2	4	6	8	10	12	14	16	18
3	3	6	9	12	15	18	21	24	27
4	4	8	12	16	20	24	28	32	36
5	5	10	15	20	25	30	35	40	45
6	6	12	18	24	30	36	42	48	54
7	7	14	21	28	35	42	49	56	63
8	8	16	24	32	40	48	56	64	72
9	9	18	27	36	45	54	63	72	81

Vedic Square

		A	B	C	D	D'	C'	B'	A'	E
		1	2	3	4	5	6	7	8	9
A	1	1	2	3	4	5	6	7	8	9
B	2	2	4	6	8	1	3	5	7	9
C	3	3	6	9	3	6	9	3	6	9
D	4	4	8	3	7	2	6	1	5	9
D'	5	5	1	6	2	7	3	8	4	9
C'	6	6	3	9	6	3	9	6	3	9
B'	7	7	5	3	1	8	6	4	2	9
A'	8	8	7	6	5	4	3	2	1	9
E	9	9	9	9	9	9	9	9	9	9

Mapping the patterns to circles that are divided into 9 parts gives you a better understanding of the patterns encoded within the Vedic Square. For example, the pattern B is 2, 4, 6, 8, 1, 3, 5, 7, 9 and it is shown below in the upper right diagram. The B' sequence runs backwards compared to B on the same diagram.

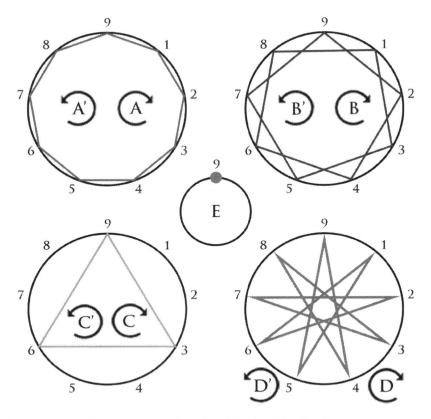

Four geometries are associated with the Vedic Square sequence plus sequence E, which is a repetition of 9, visualized as a single point of unity at the top of the circle.

Vedic Mathematics is the name for a rapid mental calculation system that utilizes the patterns within the Vedic Square among other timesaving mental visualizations. People versed in Vedic Math can perform impressive calculations almost instantly in their heads by applying 16 simple rules encoded in "sutras" or aphorisms.

See the book series <u>The Cosmic Calculator: A Vedic Mathematics Course for Schools</u> by Kenneth Williams and Mark Gaskell (2002) for more on this little-known branch of mathematical knowledge.

The patterns arising from the Vedic Square resonate with the wisdom encoded in the ancient Egyptian Ennead.

What's in a Name?

Alfred J. Parker (1897-1964) founded the Kabalarian Philosophy which assigns letters to numbers using a circle divided into 9 parts. Parker believed essentially that "you are your name" and that the letters of the alphabet are ciphers for 9 numbers.

The two basic laws of being are the numbers 1-9 and the alphabet. The first is dimension and form; the second is the symbols of the consciousness of being. Without the first there would be no physical dimension and without the second, no language, no thought, and no mind. Try to express or describe something without language; this you cannot do because all things, all objects, all pictures, must be translated into sense or intelligence. Thus does reason come into being. Contrary to many beliefs, there has always been language where there have been human beings. -
A Selection of Writings on the Kabalarian Philosophy by Alfred J. Parker (published 1975).

'What's in a Name?' by Scott Onstott

You can have your name and birth date analyzed for free at http://www.kabalarians.com

Ken Wilber's Integral Theory of Everything

Ken Wilber's Integral Theory has been called one of the most comprehensive approaches to philosophy. Building on the work of Jean Gebser, Clare Graves, Don Beck, and Chris Cowan, a fundamental aspect of Integral Theory describes 9 structures or stages of consciousness, recapitulating the historical stages of the evolution of human awareness. I find it fascinating that the structure of the human mind appears to resonate with the ennead.

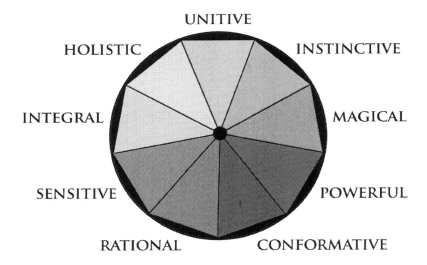

Wilber says the research shows we are all born at the Instinctive level and move sequentially clockwise as we develop. Each level transcends and includes the previous levels. Progression around the circle (or along a spiral as it is visualized in 3D) expands the number of perspectives one has to solve problems.

Here's the key idea. Different societies, cultures and subcultures, as well as entire nations are at different levels of psycho-cultural emergence, as displayed within these evolutionary levels of complexity. They have different centers of gravity. The previously awakened levels do not disappear. Rather, they stay active within the worldview stacks, thus impacting the nature and form of the more complex systems. Like the Russian dolls, there are systems within systems within systems. - "The Search for Cohesion in the

Age of Fragmentation" by Don Beck (http://bit.ly/Q46dTX)

Wilber says that the world population's center of gravity is currently in the Conformative level where "Life has meaning, direction, and purpose, with outcomes determined by an all-powerful Other or Order." -A Theory of Everything (Shambhala 2000).

There are two tiers within the theory and those in the first tier, Instinctive through Sensitive, believe that their truth is the only truth that is correct. It isn't until the second tier, Integral through Unitive, that people are able to see that all the previous stages are correct and appropriate for those who experience them.

However, Wilbur says "first-tier memes generally resist the emergence of second-tier memes." One characteristic of second-tier memes is the flexibility to appreciate the perspectives of those coming from different worldviews.

It is the mark of an educated mind to be able to entertain a thought without accepting it. -Aristotle

Second-tier stages have become aware of the evolution of consciousness itself, and this is a giant leap forward in self-awareness.

Integral theory has been applied in different domains including art, economics, politics, ecology, psychology, spirituality, and many others.

Enneagrams

G.I. Gurdjieff (1866-1949) claimed to have received an ancient teaching that was passed down through a secret brotherhood from "pre-sand Egypt" called the Enneagram. He asserted that people in their typical conscious state are actually asleep, but that it is possible to awaken and attain a fourth-dimensional super-conscious awareness through a process of self-realization that he called "The Work."

The Enneagram is the fundamental hieroglyph of a universal language. All knowledge can be included in the Enneagram and with the help of the Enneagram it can be interpreted...A man may be quite alone in the desert and he can trace the Enneagram in the sand and in it read the eternal laws of the universe. And every time he can learn something new, something he did not know before. - G.I. Gurdjieff

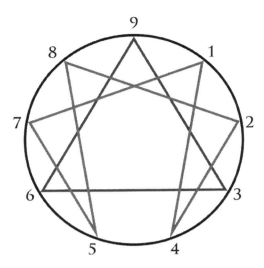

GURDJIEFF'S ENNEAGRAM

Gurjieff's Enneagram simultaneously encodes what he called the Law of Seven and the Law of Three. The Law of Seven is related to the octave in music and explains the ways energy flows in natural phenomena, in humans, and in society. Following the lines in the Enneagram, one reads the sequence 1, 4, 2, 8, 5, 7 which echoes the decimal value of $1/7 = .142857...$ All the sevenths form an interesting shifting-phase pattern that mysteriously excludes the numbers 3, 6, and 9.

$1/7 = .142857142857...$
$2/7 = .285714285714...$
$3/7 = .428571428571...$
$4/7 = .571428571428...$
$5/7 = .714285714285...$
$6/7 = .857142857142...$

All the sevenths can be traced by following the circuit that includes the numbers 1, 4, 2, 8, 5, and 7. In this sense this circuit resonates with the Law of Seven.

The Law of Three is encoded in the equilateral triangle connecting the numbers 3, 6, and 9. This law states that every whole phenomenon is composed of 3 sources that are active, passive, and reconciling. Consider the following examples of triplets:

Proton, electron, neutron;
Solid, liquid, gas;
Rational, irrational, transcendental;
Affirmation, denial, reconciliation;
Osiris, Set, Isis.

I noticed that the Law of Three, the Law of Seven, and the Enneagram are echoed in the numerology of the One Ring in The Lord of the Rings (1955):

> *Three Rings for the Elven-kings under the sky,*
>
> *Seven for the Dwarf-lords in their halls of stone,*
>
> *Nine for Mortal Men doomed to die,*
>
> *One for the Dark Lord on his dark throne*
>
> *In the Land of Mordor where the Shadows lie.*
>
> *One Ring to rule them all, One Ring to find them,*
>
> *One Ring to bring them all and in the darkness bind them.*
>
> *-J.R.R. Tolkien*

Perhaps the unseen villain Sauron was able to "rule them all" remotely from Mordor with his psychological knowledge of the Enneagram. As of the date I am writing these words (amazingly on 10/11/12), a search for the term "Enneagram" at amazon.com returns 365 results, almost all of which are psychology books.

For further evidence that Tolkien was interested in numerology consider the following quote regarding Bilbo's party in the beginning of the ring cycle:

Bilbo was going to be eleventy-one, 111, a rather curious number, and a very respectable age for a hobbit (the Old Took himself had only reached 130); and Frodo was going to be thirty-three, 33, an important number: the date of his 'coming of age.'

According to Sir Laurence Gardner in Realm of the Ring Lords

(Fair Winds Press 2002),

The Anunnaki overlords were said to have governed by way of a Grand Assembly of nine councilors who sat at Nippur. The nine consisted of eight members (seven males and a female), who held the rings of divine justice, along with their president, Anu, who held the One Ring to bind them all. Not only does this conform with the nine kingdoms of the Vosunga Saga, which cites Odin (Wotan) as the ultimate presidential Ring Lord, but it is also commensurate with the seven archangels of Hebraic record along with their two supervisors, the Lord of the Spirits and the Most High (equivalent to Anu). As the original god-kings of Mesopotamia, this Assembly was said to have introduced kingly practice which, according to the Sumerian King List (dating before 2000 BC) was 'lowered from heaven'.

If Tolkien's <u>The Lord of the Rings</u> is a story of our own psychological Middle-Earth in terms of our belief in being bound by an all-powerful Other or Order, then perhaps that is why it is one of the best-selling sagas ever written. This role-based, mythological belief system resonates with a large portion of the population according to Ken Wilber's research.

The "one ring that brings them all and in the darkness binds them" is an allegory of our collective shadow, our belief in kingship, democracy, socialism, corporatism, or any kind of "authority" other than ourselves. We must collectively throw the belief in the one ring that binds us back into Mount Doom and unmake it if we are to "come of age" and ever be free.

Kevin McMahon illustrated a resonance between the structure of the Earth's outer and inner cores, the Enneagram, and the "sharp" nine-pointed star. The resonance with these Enneagrams and the literal "Middle-Earth" is astounding.

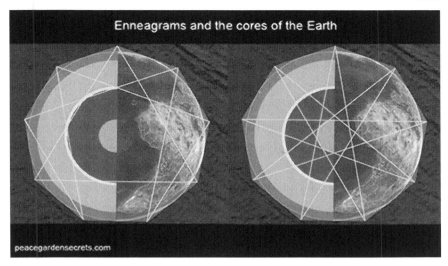

Illustration by Kevin McMahon

The Lotus Temple in Delhi is the mother temple of the Baha'i Faith in India. It is a strikingly beautiful nine-sided structure emulating a lotus flower, traditionally symbolizing the chakras. Amazingly, and quite fittingly, it receives more visitors than the Eiffel Tower and the Taj Mahal at an average of 9 persons every minute, round the clock. It is a temple open to people of all religions, expressing the architecture of the mind, the literal Middle-Earth, and much else besides.

Image of the Lotus Temple by Vandelizer under the Creative Commons Attribution 2.0 Generic license.

Visionary thinker Marko Rodin discovered what he calls "the mathematical fingerprint of God" from his decoding of the scripture of his Baha'i Faith, whose symbol happens to be a nine-pointed star. In fact Baha'i scripture specifies that every House of Worship must feature a nine-sided great room because the "Most Great" name of the Baha'i prophet reduces to 9 in the Abjad system (similar to Hebrew gematria).

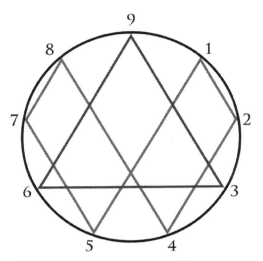

MATHEMATICAL FINGERPRINT
OF GOD BY MARKO RODIN

Rodin's *fingerprint* is correspondingly based on a circle divided into 9 parts. Rodin identifies three patterns in the fingerprint: the number 9, the sequence 1, 2, 4, 8, 7, 5 which is connected in a doubling/halving circuit, and the oscillation between 3 and 6. This tripartite classification mirrors Gurdjieff's Law of Three.

Rodin's patterns arise from the digital roots of doubling or halving any number.

DOUBLING

1	1	3	3	5	5	7	7	9	9
2	2	6	6	10	1	14	5	18	9
4	4	12	3	20	2	28	1	27	9
8	8	24	6	40	4	56	2	36	9
16	7	48	3	80	8	112	4	45	9
32	5	96	6	160	7	224	8	54	9
64	1	192	3	320	5	448	7	63	9
128	2	384	6	640	1	896	5	72	9
256	4	768	3	1280	2	1792	1	81	9
512	8	1536	6	2560	4	3584	2	90	9
1024	7	3072	3	5120	8	7168	4	99	9
2048	5	6144	6	10240	7	14336	8	108	9

HALVING

1	1	3	3	5	5	7	7	9	9
0.5	5	1.5	6	2.5	7	3.5	8	4.5	9
0.25	7	0.75	3	1.25	8	1.75	4	2.25	9
0.125	8	0.375	6	0.625	4	0.875	2	1.125	9
0.0625	4	0.1875	3	0.3125	2	0.4375	1	0.5625	9
0.03125	2	0.09375	6	0.15625	1	0.21875	5	0.28125	9

*9 is the Most Great Name of God, or primal point of unity...The 1,2,4,8,7,5 is the third dimension electric circuit while the oscillation between the 3 and 6 demonstrates the fourth dimension, which is the higher dimensional magnetic field of an electrical coil. The 3, 9, and 6 always occur together with the 9 as the control...Numbers are real and alive...For example, physics **is** the base ten number system. -Marko Rodin*

Rodin constructed an electromagnetic coil by winding it with conductive wires in a way that mapped "the mathematical fingerprint of God" onto the surface of a torus. Rodin's coil has proven to be one of the most sensitive antennas ever tested in a laboratory. Rodin claims this coil is the key to producing unlimited free energy and is the core of a future propulsion system.

If you only knew the magnificence of the three, the six, and the nine then you would have a key to the universe. -Nikola Tesla, the father of alternating electrical current

Perhaps anything is possible if one mirrors the deep numerical structure of reality in external technology. By intelligently combining knowledge of the Vedic Square, the Enneagram, and Rodin's "vortex based mathematics", these claims might one day bear fruit.

Fruit from the Tree of Knowledge

Speaking of fruit, the apple Eve picked off the mythological tree of knowledge contained a secret that I hinted at in Chapter 4 - The Honeycomb and the Apple when I wrote, "The secret of the apple can be revealed to anyone who slices the fruit in half across its equator. Every apple conceals a pentagram, a secret in plain sight."

The way to read the diagram is with 0 degrees pointed true north and by measuring angles clockwise. The first inner point is at 36 degrees, and the first outer point is at 72 degrees. Continuing on in this way, a full circle is 360 degrees and the next point is 396 degrees (360+36). As you spin around the apple you naturally hit numerous key numbers.

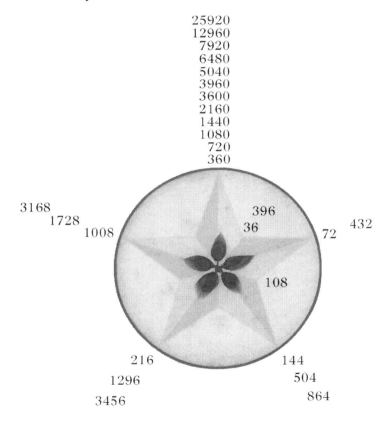

The precessional numbers are based on the traditional value of 25,920 years for the Great Year. Half of the Great Year is 12,960

years, and one-quarter of this cycle is 6,480 years. A great many myths from cultures around the world encode precessional numbers as shown in <u>Hamlet's Mill</u> by Giorgio de Santillana and Hertha Von Dechend (1969).

If you accept that the Great Year is actually 24,000 years according to Cruttenden's Binary Companion Theory (see Chapter 3 - Measuring Time), then dividing the Great Year by 360 degrees gives an average of 66.6666... years for the Earth to precess through each degree in our solar system's great cycle with the Sirius system.

Steve Jobs and Steve Wozniak sold the original Apple-1 computer for $666.66. Perhaps having invoked the so-called Devil's number, it should be no surprise that in the arc of his life, Jobs went from selling the Apple-1 out of a garage with Woz to running the world's largest publically traded corporation by market capitalization.

At Jobs' death in 2011, Apple Computer was the largest technology company in the world by revenue and profit, earning more than Google and Microsoft combined. In 2011 Apple earned $108 billion in revenue and had $33 billion in operating income with financial reserves exceeding those of the US Government (and most other governments in the world).

*****

Plato is credited for the discovery of the five regular convex polyhedra, the so-called Platonic solids. However, carved stone models of these five forms have been found in Neolithic ruins, which date at least a millennium before Plato. The Neo-platonic philosopher Proclus credited Pythagoras with the discovery of these five forms. Whoever is ultimately credited, humans have been aware of these five three-dimensional forms since pre-dynastic Egypt.

Amazingly, the sums of all the angles in the Platonic solids are encoded in the forbidden fruit. Compare the following numbers to the illustration above (they are all there):

Dodecahedron = 6480 degrees
Icosahedron = 3600 degrees
Cube = 2160 degrees

Octahedron = 1440 degrees
Tetrahedron = 720 degrees

Traditional "Imperial" measures encode more of the numbers (thanks to Randall Carlson):

1 square foot = 144 square inches
1 square yard = 1296 square inches
1 cubic foot = 1728 cubic inches

John Michell's canonical numbers relating to the cosmos are likewise encoded in the 5-fold symmetry of the Apple:

1,080 miles, radius of Moon
2,160 miles, diameter of Moon
3,960 miles, radius of Earth
5,040 miles, combined radii of Moon and Earth
7,920 miles, diameter of Earth
432,000 miles, radius of the Sun
864,000 miles, diameter of the Sun

In addition, the doubling sequence 108, 216, 432, 864, 1728, 3456 is also encoded, tying in with Hindu chronology. Even 10:08 is in there.

At a deeper level, consider the fact that every one of the numbers cycling around the apple has the digital root of 9—fruit of the gods indeed!

Chapter 7 - Taxonomy of Encoded Structures

After finding numerous examples of encoded structures all over the world, I have created a system of classification to help others perceive *secrets in plain sight* in their own backyards or anywhere in the world using tools such as Google Earth.

This chapter will give examples illustrating each of the five classifications within this taxonomy.

Encoded Design

Architecture and urban design is very often encoded with symbols, sacred geometry, numbers, and/or is specifically designed to resonate with the human body.

There is a powerful need for symbolism, and that means the architecture must have something that appeals to the human heart. -Kenzo Tange, architect

The Mausoleum of Halicarnassus, one of the 7 wonders of the ancient world, inspired Los Angeles City Hall. It has 32 floors and is located between Main and Temple streets. As such it is the main temple for the civic life of Los Angeles.

The concrete of the tower was mixed with sand from each of California's 58 counties and water from each of its historical Spanish Missions.

Sir James George Frazer explained the two types of sympathetic magic in The Golden Bough (1890):

If we analyze the principles of thought on which magic is based, they will probably be found to resolve themselves into two: first, that like produces like, or that an effect resembles its cause; and, second, that things which have once been in contact with each other continue to act on each other at a distance after the physical contact has been severed. The former principle may be called the Law of Similarity, the latter the Law of Contact or Contagion. From the first of these principles, namely the Law of Similarity, the magician infers that he can produce any effect he desires merely by imitating it: from the second he infers that whatever he does to a material object will affect equally the person with whom the object was once in contact, whether it formed part of his body or not.

The Doctrine of Signatures derives from the Law of Similarity wherein herbs, fruits, and vegetables that resemble various parts of the human body turn out to be specifically well suited to treating ailments in those parts.

The Signatures likewise are taken notice of, they being as it were the Books out of which the Ancients first learned the Vertues of Herbes; Nature or rather the God of nature, having stamped on divers of them legible Characters to discover their uses. - William Coles, Adam in Eden (1657)

For example, tomatoes and red peppers are good for the heart (4 chambers, red), kidney beans are good for the kidneys (matching shape and color), walnuts are good for the brain (two hemispheres joined by narrow bridge and highly convoluted), celery is good for bones (long, light, and strong), and so on. This philosophy was common in ancient Greece and Rome and it has been revived and suppressed many times since then. Paracelsus said, "it is not in the quantity of food but in its quality that resides the spirit of life."

There are two forms of sympathetic magic at work in the City of Angels' Civic Temple. First the likeness of the building to the ancient wonder of the world resonates with its mythological power by the Law of Similarity. Incidentally the original Mausoleum of Halicarnassus was surrounded by 36 columns and capped off by a pyramid of 24 steps.

Secondly, embedding physical substances (sand and water) from all the counties of California and from the legacy of Spanish Missions connects the building to the region and the past by the Law of Contact or Contagion.

The House of the Temple, officially known as "Home of The Supreme Council, 33°, Ancient & Accepted Scottish Rite of Freemasonry, Southern Jurisdiction, Washington D.C., U.S.A." was intentionally designed as another replica of the Mausoleum of Halicarnassus and serves as the tomb of Albert Pike, Confederate General and the most famous freemason in his day. Pike wrote Morals and Dogma, a handbook detailing the degrees in the Scottish Rite.

The nearby 333 foot high George Washington National Masonic Memorial in Alexandria, Virginia is a replica of the Lighthouse of Alexandria, Egypt.

Masonic Center at 1111 California Street in San Francisco officially contains gravel and soil from each of California's 58 counties. Masons appear to understand the principles of magic.

The classical architectural style itself encodes subtle lessons in its grammar. Daniel Tatman explains that the clean lines of a Doric column represent an initiate just beginning a personal journey of self-realization. The Ionic order with its stylized scrolls represents study and the assimilation of knowledge (the "work"). The ornate Corinthian order's elegant scrolls and acanthus leaves represent the flowering of knowledge into wisdom. I see the shaft of the Corinthian order's 24 flutes and its column, which is 10 diameters high as encoding cycles of time and the decimal system through its architectural details and proportions.

Building dimensions can also be used to encode layers of meaning. For example, professor of architecture Keith Critchlow showed how Chartres Cathedral's Sun tower being 365 feet high and its Moon tower being 28 feet lower resonates with the solar year and lunar sidereal month. See the DVD "Chartres Cathedral – A Sacred Geometry" (2000 Golden Age).

I noticed that Paris' Eiffel Tower is 320 meters tall, the height of an 81-story building. The top floor is at a height of 273 meters. These are all key numbers.

Hearst Tower near Columbus circle in Midtown Manhattan encodes many key solar numbers. Designed by world famous architect Sir Norman Foster, it is the headquarters of the Hearst Corporation and was the first skyscraper to break ground after 9/11. Its 864,000 square foot floor area (99.7%) resonates with the Sun's 864,000 mile diameter (99.9%). The exterior structure of the building has 216 equilateral triangles and 36 isosceles triangles. $216 = 6 \times 6 \times 6$ and the sum of the numbers 1-36 is 666.

As mentioned in Chapter 5 - Key Numbers, the magic square of the Sun has rows and columns adding up to 666. The encodings in the Hearst Tower therefore triply resonate with the Sun.

Singular works of architecture can, through sympathetic magic's

Law of Similarity, resonate with the human body. For example Chartres Cathedral encodes the human form both in the building elevation and in its floor plan, as illustrated in Secrets In Plain Sight - Volume 1.

In terms of an architectural complex encoding a number by design, consider the fact that the sum of the heights of all the buildings in the new World Trade Center in New York is 6660 feet. See my blog posts http://bit.ly/PZ7igN and http://bit.ly/OJ19Ea for more information.

Much can be encoded in the layout of streets and in the design of formal architectural complexes on the scale of cities. One such example is Astana Kazakhstan.

Astana has a central axis or spine. I overlaid Leonardo da Vinci's Vitruvian Man, the most famous depiction of the human body ever made, over Astana. The Roman architect Vitruvius' Ten Books of Architecture (15 BC) describe how effective temples encode the proportions of the human body.

Sir Norman Foster designed the end structure of the Astana axis, with in the Palace of Peace and Reconciliation at the crown chakra and the aptly named Khan Shatyr Entertainment Center corresponding to the sexual energy chakra at the other end of Astana's spine. Bayterek, the name of the tower centered on the heart chakra, is the most famous symbol of Astana. Bayterek is a world tree with a 22-meter diameter sphere in its branches symbolizing the golden egg laid by the mythological Samruk bird, the Kazakh phoenix.

Through the Law of Similarity the urban body of Astana resonates with the bodies of the individual residents and visitors who tour the city: as above, so below.

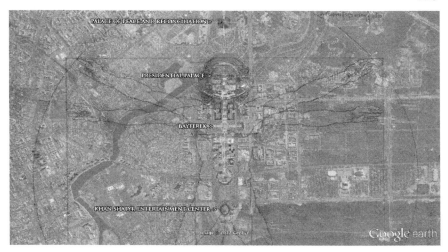

The Presidential Palace is appropriately located at the third-eye chakra at the center of the encoded body's head. The center of the dome of the Presidential Palace is 3,300,000 yards from the Ishtar gate of ancient Babylon, wonder of the ancient world.

Coincidentally Craig Compton, a fan of my work, pointed out that a reconstruction of the Ishtar Gate and Processional Way in Berlin's Pergamon Museum is 3,333 km from the original Ishtar Gate in Babylon.

I discovered that the root chakra at the endpoint of the Astana axis is 4,444,444 yards from the center of the Great Pyramid in Egypt.

Incredibly, in Astana, a giant phoenix is depicted in the landscaping above the top of the Vitruvian man's head, flying toward the crown chakra at the Palace of Peace and Reconciliation, a symbolic holy spirit in flight.

The Palace of Peace and Reconciliation was specially constructed to host the "Congress of Leaders of World Religions" containing accommodations for spiritual leaders from Judaism, Christianity, Islam, Buddhism, Hinduism, and other faiths. The religious delegates sit around a large central table with 32 arrows around its circumference pointing in towards a solar symbol at the center. It is a Pyramid of One World Religion, as the structure is literally a 4-sided pyramid. At the top of the pyramid doves are depicted in the stained glass, Astana's birds of peace and reconciliation.

Doves are in the genus *columbidae.* from the Latin *columba* meaning dove. The District of Columbia in the United States echoes these birds of peace. Ironically, DC is the headquarters of the highest funded military in the history of the world ($550 billion spent in 2011 alone).

The pyramid form can be used as a symbol of control from the top down and presumably any attempt to create a one world religion could lead to a tyranny of belief. The pyramid in Astana that assembles "leaders of world religions" stands in stark contrast to the Lotus Temple in New Delhi which acts instead as "a gathering place where people of all religions may worship without denominational restrictions."

There are many more layers of symbolism encoded by design in Astana that I blogged about here: http://bit.ly/OE0F26.

Encoded Location

What are the top three most important considerations in real estate? Location, location, and location. Built structures can encode information by virtue of their location upon the Earth. The examples in this section will show how location can be used to encode key numbers, physical constants, and even the slope of the Great Pyramid.

The center of Saddam Hussein's reconstruction of ancient Babylon is at latitude 32 deg 32 min 32 sec North.

The Chet Holifield Federal Building in southern California is located at 33 deg 33 min 33 sec North. William Pereira, the same architect who designed the Transamerica Pyramid in San Francisco, designed it.

The Holifield building is known locally as "The Ziggurat" because, by the Law of Similarity, its design was encoded to have the same seven-stepped form of the original Babylonian ziggurat called Etemenanki, home of the god Marduk. The Department of Homeland Security has a home on the seventh floor of this US ziggurat.

There is another modern ziggurat in London, in the MI6 building, which is colloquially known as Babylon-on-the-Thames because it too was designed to mimic the Babylonian ziggurat. It is an interesting coincidence that both governments chose to house secret intelligence agencies inside ziggurats.

For knowledge itself is power. -Francis Bacon

In Chapter 2 - Metrology I mentioned a couple of encoded locations:

The latitude of the Great Pyramid (GP) encodes the speed of light in meters/second.

The speed of light is 299,792,458 meters/second.
The latitude of GP is 29.9792458 degrees North.

The latitude of the original location of the London Stone is 51.5114 deg N. This is amazing because the slope angle of the Great Pyramid is 51 deg 51 min 14 sec, as measured from its few remaining casing stones.

Also in New York City, the building formerly known as Freedom Tower (now One World Trade Center) is located at the following decimal coordinates:

40.713 deg latitude
-74.013 deg longitude

In decimal coordinates, latitudes north of the equator and longitudes east of the prime meridian are positive. Doing the math, 40.713 - 74.013 = -33.300.

The One World Trade Center is 1776 feet high or 888 + 888 feet, so it encodes on the design level as well. The structure is like two Transamerica Pyramids intersecting as above so below if you will, resting on a cubical base. The midpoint of the tower has an octagonal floor plate, a solar symbol. See my blog post http://bit.ly/O56Npj for more on this particular structure.

In summary, you have learned a variety of methods for how latitude and longitude can encode key numbers.

Encoded Orientation

The orientation of structures to true North can be a code connecting them to other structures or key numbers. The design, location, and orientation work together in determining what the complex is pointing to in the distance. The following examples illustrate some of the many ways the orientation of architectural structures and urban complexes can be encoded with hidden knowledge.

The ancient Egyptian Temple of Amen at Karnak is an immense quarter million square meter complex that is symmetric about a central axis. The sunrise on the winter solstice appears perfectly on this axis, framed between the architectural pylons of the temple. This of course reveals that the complex was designed to encode this particular orientation, which is to be expected for a solar temple.

A complex directly across the Nile at the Theban necropolis, the Mortuary Temple of Hatshepsut, is likewise oriented in the same direction, to the azimuth of winter solstice sunrise. It should be no surprise then that this temple was likewise dedicated to the Sun god Amen.

In Chapter 3 - Measuring Time I mentioned that the axis of Notre Dame in Paris and the Champs Elysees are oriented to the heliacal rising of Sirius, the phenomenon the ancient Egyptians based their new year on.

In addition to pointing to the Sun or Sirius, complexes can be oriented to other complexes on the Earth. This can be verified by drawing the shortest path between two sites and seeing if the heading is a key number or by projecting lines suggested by the architectural design out into the landscape and seeing if the lines cross over any structures of significance.

For example, a path drawn from the Dome of the Rock in Jerusalem to the Hagia Sophia in Istanbul has a heading of 333 degrees true North.

The Dome of the Rock is sacred to all three Abrahamic religions and the bedrock at its heart is considered by many to be the place where Moses nearly sacrificed Isaac/Ishmael, to be the location of the holy of holies within the destroyed Temple of Solomon, and the place where Mohammed ascended into heaven accompanied by the archangel Gabriel.

The Hagia Sophia (meaning Shrine of the Holy Wisdom) was the largest cathedral in the world for more than 1,000 years and served as a mosque for almost 500 years before being converted to the museum that it is today. It is the epitome of Byzantine architecture as such is said to have changed the history of architecture.

The path connecting these sites passes from the center of the Dome of the Rock through one of the corners of its octagonal structure. This correlation with the architectural design adds another layer to the significance of this heading angle of 333 degrees. The sites are also both world heritage sites with great religious, cultural, and historical significance. Obviously reading meaning into an encoded orientation line is more plausible when the endpoints themselves are hugely significant.

Encoded Distance

Distances between monuments sometimes encode numbers that suggest planning. In Chapter 2 - Metrology you learned that Imperial and Metric measures are rooted in cosmic harmonies with the Earth, Moon, Sun, and the speed of light. Therefore you are free to measure using a variety of units and can rest assured that these numbers resonate within the larger system of which we are all a part.

When you are measuring distances, accuracy and precision are paramount. If you are using Google Earth to measure it is necessary to zoom in closely to each endpoint and position the virtual cord you are stretching over the surface of the Earth as carefully as possible.

Obviously the more significant the endpoints are, the more meaning one might ascribe to an encoded distance between them. It probably doesn't matter if is it is 333 meters between the grocery store and the hairdressers to anyone save for the residents of a particular village. However, sacred measures can and are used at every scale.

A garden bed measuring 5 by 12 feet has an area of 8640 square inches, resonating with the Sun's diameter of 864,000 miles (99.9%).

The 35mm film format used for over 100 years, which continues today with full frame digital SLR cameras, measures 36mm x 24 mm, having an area of 864 square millimeters. This is the most appropriate size to capture the light of the Sun in this small scale.

The following examples are of longer encoded distances:

Jan Thulstrup discovered that the distance from Columbus Tower, London (under construction in Canary Wharf) to Columbus Tower, San Francisco (at the base of the Transamerica Pyramid) is 8640 kilometers. He also noted that the spire of Notre Dame in Paris to the center of Rosslyn Chapel in Scotland is 864 kilometers.

Michell and Heath showed in The Lost Science of Measuring the Earth that the distance between Stonehenge and Silbury Hill is 86,400 feet and that Silbury Hill was designed using whole units of 8.64 feet.

Mark Gray (cosmicdoorways.net) discovered that the distance from the tip of the pyramid on the tallest building in the World Financial Center in New York City (across the street from One World Trade Center) to Cleopatra's Needle in Central Park is 333,000 inches.

I looked into Disneyland Paris and discovered it is inscribed in a circle with a diameter of 3141 meters, recalling Pi. The distance from the center of the Disneyland circle to the tip of the Louvre Pyramid is 33033 meters. Disneyland's mysterious Club 33 also springs to mind.

The distance from Nelson's column in Trafalgar Square to the center of London Olympic Stadium is 33,333 inches.

The distance from the center of the London Olympic Stadium to the center of the oldest round structure of Temple Church (built by the Knights Templar) is 7,770 yards.

The distance from the center of Temple Round Church to the center of the tower atop Freemasons' Hall is 864 yards. Freemasons' Hall (opened in 1933) is the headquarters of the United Grand Lodge of England; it is located on Great Queen Street, recalling Isis.

Kevin McMahon (peacegardensecrets.com) discovered that the distance from the Pyramid of Peace and Reconciliation in Astana is 8880 kilometers from the Peace Towers in the International Peace Garden on the US/Canada border. Both complexes are more or less at the centers of their respective continents. The ancient magical practice of establishing the center point of a land mass as a world axis or omphalos, and measuring distances relative to that point is described in Twelve Tribe Nations: Sacred Number and the

Golden Age by John Michell and Christine Rhone (Inner Traditions 1991).

I noticed that the heading from the Palace of Peace and Reconciliation to the Peace Towers in the International Peace Garden is 354.36 degrees true North. The lunar year is 354.36 days.

The distance from the golden Dome of the Rock to the Adam's apple (remember the garden of Eden?) of Astana's encoded man is 3652.42 km, echoing the solar year of 365.242 days.

As you can see there are numerous encoded distances revealing a metrological structure to reality. Finding these distances is a team effort. Anyone with Internet access can download the free version of Google Earth and do research in this area.

Encoded Alignment

In Secrets In Plain Sight - Volume 1 I discussed the significance of the ancient Egyptian Temple of Dendur inside the Metropolitan Museum of Art in New York City in how it is part of an alignment. This Isis temple is in line with a linear structure under the waters of the Jacqueline Kennedy Onassis reservoir in Central Park. The alignment passes through the ancient Egyptian Temple of Dendur, and continues straight to the United Nations headquarters building on the East River.

Two other similar ancient temples were given to Spain and Italy just before the Aswan Dam was built in Upper Egypt in the 1960s, called Debod and Ellesyia respectively. The Temple of Debod was relocated to Madrid. The linear axis of the Debod complex in Madrid points directly to the ancient Egyptian obelisk in St. Peter's Square.

To trace this alignment yourself in Google Earth begin by zooming into the Temple of Debod in Madrid (40.424040°N, 3.717774°W). Draw a line from left to right along the central axis of the complex and take a note of its bearing angle, which is 77.7 degrees in this case. Type Vatican in the search box and you will fly there. Zoom into St. Peter's Square and click the endpoint of the cord you are stretching across the globe on the center of the Vatican obelisk. Do you see how it runs through the middle of the Vatican's linear axis and crosses the W wind rose marker surrounding the obelisk? This axial alignment with both linear complexes suggests intentional design or is simply an incredible coincidence.

The Temple of Ellesyia (45.068402°N, 7.684414°E) is located in the Museo Egizio in Turin, which houses the world's largest collection of Egyptian antiquities outside Cairo. Drawing a line from this museum to the Vatican obelisk reveals that this path also crosses a wind rose marker; in this case it is the NW stone.

Cort Lindahl discovered additional significant alignments passing through wind rose markers surrounding the Vatican obelisk in his book <u>Geomantic Information Systems Volume 1</u> (Createspace 2010). These include Aachen Cathedral in Germany to the NNW, Schonbrunn Palace in Vienna to the NNE, the Hagia Sophia in Istanbul to the E, and the Dome of the Rock in Jerusalem to the ESE. Lindahl sees the Vatican obelisk as an axis mundi or world axis.

Byzantium (Istanbul) was the capital of the Roman Empire in late antiquity. In the Middle Ages Holy Roman Emperors ruled in Aachen and later in Schonbrunn. The double-headed eagle was the emblem of Byzantium and the Holy Roman Emperors and remains today the emblem of Scottish Rite freemasonry.

Lindahl's approach is to study the lines suggested by architecture and project them out into the landscape. He discovered the alignments surrounding the Vatican obelisk by tracing paths through the various wind rose markers and seeing if they pass through significant sites.

Another fascinating example of this type of alignment is Lindahl's projection of lines from the Great Pyramid's square base. He drew the diagonals of this square and saw that the NW line passes through the 32-story Pyramid Arena in Memphis Tennessee, a city which was of course named after the ancient Egyptian capital. The NE line passes through the hexagonal temple of Baalbek in Lebanon. The SE line passes through the Kaaba in Mecca, Saudi Arabia.

Another type of alignment is one that passes through 3 points. For example, I discovered an alignment from Bourges cathedral in France, through Freemasons' Hall in London that houses the

United Grand Lodge of England, continuing to Rosslyn chapel in Scotland. This alignment resonates with Bernard de Clairvaux as the seminal figure in the founding of the Cistercian and Templar orders and the subsequent flowering of the Gothic style that he helped to inspire.

The Templar tradition ties in with Rosslyn chapel that has depictions of maize, a new world crop, carved a century before Columbus reached America.

There is a growing body of evidence suggesting the Cistercians colonized America long before Columbus sailed under the Templar flag. (Read The Kensington Runestone by Scott Wolter).

Jim Alison (http://home.hiwaay.net/~jalison/) has identified a number of great circles passing all the way around the Earth on which many sacred sites are located. For example there is a single great circle connecting Giza, Machupicchu, Nazca, Easter Island, Mohenjo Daro, Ur, Petra, and 10 more sacred sites around the world.

Another of Alison's great circle alignments connects Nazca, Angkor Wat, and San Francisco. In fact the great circle runs right down Columbus Avenue and passes through the Transamerica Pyramid. Angkor Wat was the largest Hindu temple complex in the world. It was first dedicated to Vishnu and centuries later it was rededicated to Buddha. The modern name Angkor Wat means "Temple City." The azimuth of the great circle parallels the azimuth of one of the Nazca plain's major lines etched into the desert floor. Angkor and Nazca are antipodal sites meaning they are halfway around the world from each other. San Francisco's location divides this half circle at the Phi point.

Jean Richer discovered a *rhumb line* (introduced in Chapter 2 - Metrology) starting at Mount Carmel in Israel that passes through Delos, Athens, Delphi, Bourges cathedral, Mont St. Michel, St. Michael's Mount, and 8 more sacred sites all the way to Ireland. All of the sites are dedicated either to Apollo the Sun god, or the archangel Michael, a name that means, "who is like God" in Hebrew. This discovery was profiled in Twelve Tribe Nations: Sacred Number and the Golden Age.

As you have seen there are many ways sites can be aligned on the

Earth and to the heavens. Alignments can be the most complex encoding systems using combinations of design, location, orientation, and/or distances.

Chapter 8 - Encoded Structures

This chapter will take you on a tour of encoded structures by picking up a theme and discovering where it leads. You can take endless journeys such as this once you train yourself with "eyes to see and ears to hear" with the tools presented in the previous 7 chapters.

I will start with the curious fact that the armistice that ended the First World War went into effect on the 11th hour of the 11th day of the 11th month. This has been celebrated as Remembrance Day ever since. The strange thing is the armistice was signed in a train car between 5:12 and 5:20 in the morning of 11/11/18 but the signers decided to wait and make it come into effect at 11 o'clock.

Why did we agree to all stop slaughtering each other on the 11th hour of the 11th day of the 11th month?

Remembrance Day is currently celebrated in the 52 countries that are members of the Commonwealth of Nations. The Commonwealth developed out of the old British Empire. In central London a cannon is fired when Big Ben strikes 11 o'clock on 11/11 and two minutes of silence are observed. Before this ritual begins thousands of red remembrance poppies and red wreaths representing the blood that was spilled in war are placed at the foot of *cenotaphs* throughout the Commonwealth of Nations.

The Shine of Remembrance in Melbourne (dedicated on November 11th, 1934) is another memorial to those who died in the Great War and now to all Australians who have served in any war. Its design is based on the Tomb of Mausolus at Halicarnassus and the Parthenon in Athens (perhaps a form of sympathetic magic).

At the core of the shrine is a marble slab covering the cenotaph upon which is engraved the words "Greater Love Hath No Man." A slender shaft of sunlight illuminates the word "Love" annually on 11th hour of the 11th day of the 11th month. The complex cost an equivalent of £11.1 million in today's currency.

There is an eternal flame in front of the Shrine of Remembrance. Eternal flames are symbolic of the divine spark animating the body. There was an eternal flame in front of the sanctuary of Apollo at Delphi, and another on the outer altar of Solomon's temple. In modern times we also have the Olympic eternal flame.

The Voortrekker Monument in Pretoria, South Africa resonates very strongly with the Shrine of Remembrance. Gerard Moerdijk designed the Voortreeker Monument with a central oculus in the ceiling admitting the light of the Sun which when one looks up appears as a dot within a circle (a *circumpunct,* or all-seeing-eye solar symbol). The shaft of light passes through another round opening in the floor inside which is inlaid with 32 rays of chevrons radiating from the center. The vertical shaft of light is the literal 33rd ray. The double chevron was the hieroglyph for water in ancient Egypt. The floor thus represents the watery abyss, known as Nu in ancient Egypt.

All roads on the terrain of building art lead back to ancient Egypt.
-Gerard Moerdijk

Moerdijk traveled to Egypt where he was impressed with Akhenaten's sun temples including the Mansion of the Benben at Karnak. In the Pyramid Texts (the oldest known religious texts in the world) the creation story can be summarized as follows: in the beginning the creator Atum arose out of the waters of Nu (perhaps a metaphor for space) either on or as "the primeval mound" (which may be a metaphor for the Earth). The first rays of light from the rising Sun struck a stone slab, known as a *benben*, on top of the mound. Don't forget Atum is god 1 of 9, or $1/9 = .111111...$ which fits right in with 11th hour of the 11th day of the 11th month.

In the Voortrekker Monument, the light of the Sun ultimately forms a glowing sun disc, or Aten, where it strikes the benben slab covering the cenotaph in the crypt. If one looks down from above the cenotaph it appears at the center of 32 watery chevrons within a circle that represents the boundary of the primeval mound.

Parts of this creation story were echoed thousands of years later in Christianity in the first 10 lines of the Bible:

1 In the beginning God created the heavens and the earth.

2 The earth was without form, and void; and darkness was on the face of the deep. And the Spirit of God was hovering over the face of the waters.

3 Then God said, "Let there be light"; and there was light.

4 And God saw the light, that it was good; and God divided the light from the darkness.

5 God called the light Day, and the darkness He called Night. So the evening and the morning were the first day.

6 Then God said, "Let there be a firmament in the midst of the waters, and let it divide the waters from the waters."

7 Thus God made the firmament, and divided the waters which were under the firmament from the waters which were above the firmament; and it was so.

8 And God called the firmament Heaven. So the evening and the morning were the second day.

9 Then God said, "Let the waters under the heavens be gathered together into one place, and let the dry land appear"; and it was so.

10 And God called the dry land Earth, and the gathering together of the waters He called Seas. And God saw that it was good.

The cenotaph slab says "We for Thee, South Africa" and is annually illuminated at noon on December 16th, the date of the 1840 Battle of Blood River, when Boer pioneers who left Cape Colony massacred 3,000 Zulus on the banks of the Ncome river, turning it into a "blood river." After Apartheid in 1994, December 16th was renamed from "Day of the Vow" to "Day of Reconciliation."

The Voortrekker Monument has a cubic form, 40m in each dimension that Moerdijk described as an altar. It also boasts an "eternal flame" that has been burning continuously since 1938.

Cenotaph is Greek for "empty tomb." The original empty tomb is the Osirion in Abydos Egypt, honoring Osiris as Lord of the Dead. This is where the ancient Flower of Life symbol is found reproduced twice on the stone, dated anywhere from 10,500 BCE to the 1st century CE. Some say the symbols were drawn in red ochre while author Gregg Braden claims it was "flash-burned" into the granite, see Awakening to Zero Point: The Collective Initiation (Sacred Spaces Ancient Wisdom 1995).

Sir Edwin Lutyens who also designed India Gate in New Delhi to honor the soldiers who died in WWI designed the Cenotaph in London. India Gate (unveiled 1933) is located inside a hexagonal complex.

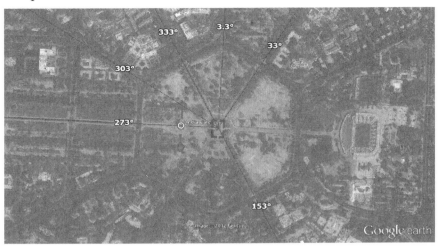

India Gate Hexagon in New Delhi

Streets radiating out of the 306,000 square meter hexagon have azimuths of 3.3, 33, 303, 333, 153, and 273 degrees – all of these are key numbers. The 273-degree azimuth leads down the Rajpath directly to Rashtrapati Bhavan, the President of India's residence (also designed by Lutyens). Underneath India Gate there is "the flame of the immortal soldier."

Sir Edwin Lutyens planned New Delhi with the assistance of Sir Herbert Baker and the foundations were laid December 15th, 1911, one day before the Day of Reconciliation in South Africa. The design is based on a triangle connecting Connaught Place with the legislative Raisina Hill and the deathly India Gate hexagon. Connaught Place is the showpiece of New Delhi featuring a central business district ringed by two circular roads perhaps symbolizing the exoteric and esoteric aspects of the design.

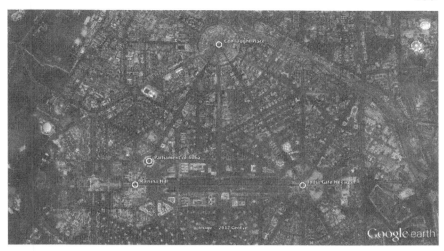

The geometric basis of New Delhi is a triangle

The New Delhi triangle has an area of 266 hectares.

In the early mythologies (such as those from Hermopolis in Egypt and from the Maori of New Zealand) the original creation of the universe is linked to the opening of an egg, much like Amma's egg [the creator god] of the Dogon. The first entities to emerge after the moment of creation are the familiar triad of gods that we previously associated with the three physical states of water...This physical representation of Amma's egg—a stone with tapered sides that comes to a point—is reminiscent of the shape of the Dogon granary: conical yet roughly pyramidal...Based on the preceding diagrams and the descriptions by Hawking of the elemental particles and forces involved in quantum mechanics, we can see that the symbolism in the Dogon deep story line relating to the 266 signs or seeds of Amma presents a stunningly accurate portrait of the [sub-atomic] component building blocks of matter as we presently know them. -The Science of the Dogon: Decoding the African Mystery Tradition by Laird Scranton (Inner Traditions 2006).

Another capital of a country with a British legacy is Canberra, located in the Australian Capital Territory. American architects Walter Burley Griffin and Marion Mahoney Griffin designed the city and construction began in 1913. The equilateral Parliamentary Triangle (or Par-Tri as it is known) has a perimeter of 8.64 km, noted by Jan Thulstrup.

The Griffins oriented the city in relation to the local peak Mt. Ainslie in what they called "the land axis." The heading from Mt. Ainslie to the Australian Parliament Building bisects the Par-Tri at 216 degrees True North. 216 = 6 x 6 x 6. The end of the spinal land axis leads to the Australian War Memorial, complete with eternal flame and Tomb of the Unknown Australian Soldier cenotaph under the central dome encoded with solar motifs.

Canberra Australia's Parliamentary Triangle and "land-axis" leading to the War Memorial

The lower right corner of the triangle is the six-sided City Hill complex where the legislative and court buildings are located. The lower left corner is the five-sided Russell Hill complex where the Australian Defense Force and the Australian-American War Memorial are located. We therefore have a 6 to 5 relationship in the two hills connected to Capital Hill in the Par-Tri.

Capital Hill is the site of Parliament House that was the most expensive building in the world at more than A$1.1 billion when construction began in 1981. Double rings that perhaps symbolize both the mundane and magical aspects of the design surround parliament House. Its position in the city plan at the top of the ParTri encodes the all-seeing-eye of the Sun, much as one sees on the US $1 bill.

Lake Burley Griffin snakes through the capital like Apophis, the serpent of chaos in ancient Egypt. Canberra's geometrical order emerges out of this serpentine chaos, echoing the 33rd degree

Scottish Rite Freemason motto *ordo ab chao,* which means, "order out of chaos."

Parliament House is a pyramidal structure topped by an 81-meter flagpole atop a metallic pyramidal support structure which itself became a national symbol of Australia. 81 is connected to atoms, Atum and the ennead.

Canberra's overall plan resembles a Christmas tree or the top three sephiroth in the Kabbalistic tree of life.

Kabbalists believe the Tree of Life to be a diagrammatic representation of the process by which the Universe came into being. On the Tree of Life, the beginning of the Universe is placed at a space above the first sephira, named Keter ("crown" in English). It is not always pictured in reproductions of the Tree of Life, but is referred to universally as Ain Soph Aur (Ain - Without, Soph - End, Aur - Light). To kabbalists, it symbolizes that point beyond which our comprehension of the origins of Being cannot go; it is considered to be an infinite nothingness out of which the first "thing" (thought of in science and the Kabbalah to be energy) exploded to create a Universe of multiple things.

Kabbalists also do not envision time and space as pre-existing, and place them at the next three stages on the Tree of Life. First is Keter, which is thought of as the product of the contraction of Ain Soph Aur into a singularity of infinite energy or limitless light. In the Kabbalah, it is the primordial energy out of which all things are created. The next stage is Chokmah, or Wisdom, which is considered to be a stage at which the infinitely hot and contracted singularity expanded forth into space and time. It is often thought of as pure dynamic energy of an infinite intensity forever propelled forth at a speed faster than light.

Next comes Binah, or Understanding, which is thought of as the primordial feminine energy, the Supernal Mother of the Universe which receives the energy of Chokmah, cooling and nourishing it into the multitudinous forms present throughout the whole cosmos. It is also seen as the beginning of Time itself. -from Wikipedia Tree_of_life_(Kabbalah) page.

Interestingly, Craig Compton drew lines from New Delhi and Canberra converging on the center of the enneagon of San

Francisco and they happen to pass through a vertex and an edge midpoint of the figure.

The enneagon of San Francisco bay

The line from Canberra to San Francisco terminates at the center of Treasure Island within a baseball diamond. Compton measured the distance from this baseball diamond to the tip of the Palace of Peace and Reconciliation in Astana and discovered it is exactly 33,000,000 feet.

Why a baseball diamond? As it turns out "America's pastime" encodes some amazing secrets in plain sight. First of all the baseball field is swept out by a compass pivoting on home plate and the bases are 90 feet apart as measured by the square.

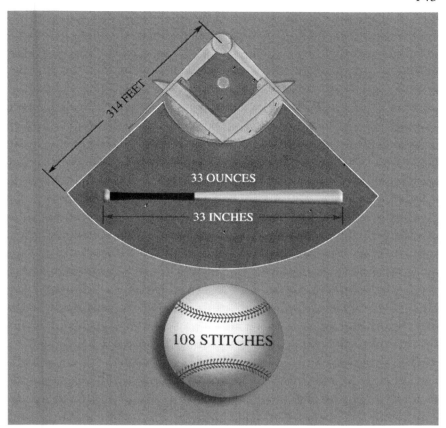

'The Sacred Geometry of Baseball' by Scott Onstott

The pitcher's mound echoes the primeval mound of creation and the pitcher symbolizes Atum, the creator god of Heliopolis. The pitcher stands on an 18 foot (9 + 9) diameter raised mound representing the primeval mound rising out of the waters of the infield (your consciousness or the microcosm). You are the batter and you get a maximum of 3 strikes or 4 balls recalling the 7 liberal arts divided into the trivium and quadrivium. Will you hit into the outfield (macrocosm) or even score a "home run" and return to the source of all things? You'll have to run the bases before you can reincarnate and bat again.

Major league baseball has 81 home games and 81 road games per season, emphasizing the number of stable atoms in the universe. 81 + 81 = 162, recalling Phi which is approximated as 1.62. There are 9 innings divided into 2 halves called top and bottom, echoing upper and lower Egypt.

The 5-sided home plate is 60'-6" away (5s and 6s) from the pitcher's plate (benben) that the pitcher must keep one foot on when he pitches. The pitcher's plate measures 24" x 6" or 144 square inches. There are 1440 minutes in 24 hours. The words "light" and "time" in Jewish gematria = 144.

The ball the pitcher throws has 108 double stitches. 108 x 2 = 216 = 6 x 6 x 6.

1080 is the Moon's radius and 2160 is the Moon's diameter in miles (99.9%).

The pitcher is the Sun throwing the Moon over the "home plate" of Earth.

An adult male of average height and weight typically selects a bat measuring 33 inches long. Baseball bats typically weigh no more than 33 ounces. The distance from home plate to right field varies from a recommended 320 feet to 400 feet (key numbers); at Yankee stadium the right field distance is 314 feet, recalling Pi which is approximated as 3.14.

It's no wonder then that baseball fans are generally the most number-obsessed of any sport! When the umpire yells "Play ball" the encoded numbers play within your psyche, regardless of whether you are conscious of it or not.

Another complex resonating with the Atum story is Cergy-Pontoise in France. Cergy-Pontoise is the name of a new town created in the 1960s; not quite an urban area, it is instead a community of 12 agglomerated villages with an area of 77.7 square kilometers.

At the end of the major axis of Cergy is a round "Astronomical Island" (primeval mound) in an artificial lake (waters of Nu). Immediately adjacent to the Astronomical Island is a small hollow pyramid partially submerged in the lake. In some versions of the Heliopolis creation myth, Atum dwelt within a small pyramid next to the primeval mound.

Philip Coppens (of Ancient Aliens TV show fame) has done some fascinating research on this complex in his essay called "Mitterand's Great – Unknown – Work" in reference to Cergy-

Pontoise (see http://bit.ly/RJDH9P). He says the small pyramid in the lake has become the breeding site for migrating birds. This is interesting considering the myth that the benu bird or phoenix roosted on the benben. The small pyramid became the prototype for pyramidions atop obelisks. According to Herodotus, there was an obelisk tipped by a benben outside the temple of the phoenix in ancient Heliopolis.

The connection between the benben, the phoenix, and the sun may well have been based on alliteration: the rising, or weben, of the sun sending its rays towards the benben, on which the benu bird lives. - Barry Kemp in Ancient Egypt: Anatomy of a Civilization (Routledge 1991)

Utterance 600 of the Pyramid Texts (circa 2400 BC) says:

O Atum, when thou didst mount as a hill, and didst shine as a benben in the temple of the phoenix in Heliopolis, and didst spew out as Shu, and did spit out as Tefnut, then thou didst put thine arms about them, as the arms of a ka [soul], that thy ka might be in them. (see http://bit.ly/Wteh9y)

After the solar Atum had arisen on the primeval mound, he masturbated (the mythmakers needed to express a solitary sexual act) and thus he created Shu, god of air, and Tefnut, goddess of moisture.

Shu and Tefnut grew up and later got together and Tefnut gave birth to Geb, god of earth, and Nut, goddess of the sky. Geb and Nut likewise bred and gave life to Set, Isis, Osiris, and Nephthys. These 9 gods comprise the Ennead.

I discovered that a line drawn from the center of Stonehenge to the spire on Notre Dame cathedral in Paris passes precisely over the center of the Astronomical Island at Cergy-Pontoise.

Cergy Pontoise alignments and distances

In addition the distance from the statue of Louis XIV in front of the Louvre pyramid to Cergy-Pontoise's Belvedere Tower described in Chapter 5 - Key Numbers is exactly 33,000 yards.

This statue of the Sun King marks the beginning of the Axe Historique (historical axis) of Paris and continues all the way to the Grand Arch in La Defense. Gianlorenzo Bernini sculpted the statue of the Sun King to appear in Hellenistic style in an imitation of Alexander the Great. Bernini is better known as the architect who designed St. Peter's Square in the Vatican.

If in early August one looks back along the historical axis from the hypercube of the Grand Arch (revealed in Secrets In Plain Sight - Volume 1) down the Champs Elysees toward the statue of the Sun King, one can observe the heliacal rising of Sirius above the statue of the Sun King just before sunrise. Paris is a masterpiece of secret architecture.

The axis of Notre Dame parallels the Axe Historique. The distance from the octagonal central spire of Notre Dame to the small pyramid in the lake next to the Astronomical Island (where Atum symbolically resides) in Cergy-Pontoise is also exactly 33,000 yards.

The Belvedere Tower marks the center point of Cergy-Pontoise where the major and minor axes come together at an angle of 133 degrees. The major axis ends in a blood red bridge that crosses the river in front of firm land in the midst of the waters, and this thin strip divides the waters of the river from the waters of the artificial lake.

There are plans to extend the bridge onto the Astronomical Island with something called *the Path* and Philip Coppens says the Astronomical Island "...is expected to see the installation of a sundial, a meridian stele, an observational staircase and various other instruments that will make this island true to its name." Coppens continues,

As mentioned, the project was conceived as one whole, yet certain sections were only constructed at a certain time. Though this would often be given logical explanations (such as funding, a special occasion, etc.), sometimes, its phased realisation resulted in higher costs. Hence, some have suggested that the project had a prescribed timeline, which was not necessarily communicated to all. Hence, though the project is often not seen as a Great Work of Mitterrand, largely because of a timeline that preceded and post-dated the French President, such purely three-dimensional considerations might be totally wrong in the realisation of a – and this – Great Work.

The minor axis runs from the Belvedere Tower through Europe's largest clock at the nearby St. Christophe train station.

I extended the minor axis of Cergy-Pontoise from the giant clock to the far north and found that it crosses the Norwegian Island of Spitsbergen, which is much closer to Greenland than Norway.

On Spitsbergen Island is Svalbard, one of the northernmost human settlements on the planet. Svalbard is the location of the Global Seed Vault ($78°14'17.39"N$, $15°26'50.06"E$) where millions of plant seeds are stored indefinitely at a temperature of $0°F$ in a bunker drilled 120 meters deep inside a mountain. The stated purpose of the Global Seed Vault is to act as a refuge for genetic material in the case of a planetary-scale catastrophe. The entrance to the Global Seed Vault is 1313 km from the North pole.

The distance from the bunker door of the Global Seed Vault to Europe's largest clock at the end of Cergy-Pontoise's minor axis is 3300 km.

Europe's largest clock resonates with Father Time, Saturn, Cronus, the grim reaper, Chronos, and ultimately Osiris as discussed in Chapter 3 - Measuring Time. Notre Dame is of course Isis, and the Astronomical Island at Cergy-Pontoise represents the home of Atum.

Ensuring that the genetic material from Earth's plant species is backed up is always good idea because extinction is forever. However, imagining a catastrophe on a planetary scale where a vault deep within a mountain at Svalbard would be needed to reboot agriculture at some unknown point in the future is very unsettling.

I never would have predicted that the trail would start with Remembrance Day and end with envisioning the future but perhaps it is fitting that we end this journey now that we have come around the spiral directly above the point where we started.

Chapter 9 - Behind the Curtain

In the previous chapters we have followed various means of taking measure of the universe, starting with the decimal system, proceeding to units of measure encoding key numbers and cycles of time, understanding the importance of the 6 to 5 relationship, identifying key numbers around which disparate phenomena converge, perceiving patterns emerging from number, classifying the different ways this knowledge is encoded in built structures, and taking a journey examining synchronicity in encoded structures. This journey leads us now to a single underlying concept, *the principle of resonance*.

Resonance occurs when a system is able to transfer energy between two different modes. These modes span acoustic, optical, mechanical, electrical, orbital, and molecular realms, resonating all the way from the atomic scale up to the planetary scale and beyond. I speculate that the universal principle of resonance can even be extended to non-physical modes operating in higher dimensions.

If you pluck a single violin string it will vibrate at its resonant frequency based on the force applied to the string, the string length, and its tension. String tension and air resistance slowly dampen the energy mechanically stored in the oscillating standing wave. The amazing thing isn't so much the physics of the single vibrating string but how the vibrating string induces sympathetic vibrations in all the other violin strings at harmonic frequencies related to the plucked string's fundamental tone. One instrument can even induce resonance in other instruments nearby. Resonance reveals that the musicians and the audience are all connected. We hear music because the standing waves in the air resonate our eardrums and we appreciate the tune if it resonates with us internally. Appreciating music is therefore a cascade of resonances.

By the principle of resonance, a different mode or modes (in this case air and the wooden structure of the violin) transfer energy from the plucked string to other strings. This resonance induces the non-plucked strings to respond with harmonic standing waves, even though the musician has not touched them.

In essentially two-dimensional mediums such as a metal plate covered with flour (17th century Chaldni plates) or a wide glass container filled to shallow depth with a viscous liquid (as in the case of the contemporary CymaScope instrument), audible standing waves can induce ordered geometries to appear in the medium, sometimes with surprising complexity and near perfect symmetry. Order can appear magically out of chaos.

The slow adjustment of the vibration frequency on Chaldni plates or in the CymaScope (see cymascope.com) reveals that the standing wave geometry appears to be a sectional slice through an invisible three-dimensional form. Sound is geometry and geometry is crystallized sound.

I call architecture frozen music. -Johann Wolfgang von Goethe

Cymatics is the name given to the science of the resonance between sound and form and was named by the Swiss doctor and pioneer Hans Jenny (1904-1972).

Cymatic forms look much like many of the crop circle designs that have been appearing with increasing frequency in the fields of Southern England every summer near Stonehenge, Avebury, and Silbury Hill.

Two NASA spacecraft recorded an immense persistent cymatic standing wave pattern larger than the Earth appearing in the viscous atmosphere of Saturn's north polar region as mentioned in Chapter 2 - Metrology.

Richard Hoagland (enterprisemission.com) has shown how star tetrahedron geometry is implicated in energy outflows coming from planetary cores in our solar system. When a star tetrahedron is inscribed within a sphere, its points touch the sphere's surface at 19.47 degrees north and south latitude.

Hoagland theorizes that one of the tetrahedral points is on the Mauna Loa volcano in Hawaii, which is actually the largest mountain on Earth if measured from the sea floor. He also found similar energy outflows occurring at 19.47 degrees north or south on Mars' Olympus Mons (which is the largest mountain in the solar system), in Jupiter's Great Red Spot, and Neptune's Great Dark Spot.

Explaining these outflows requires a four-dimensional model of physics where energy is gated from the Sun to the planetary cores through hyperspace. Energy resonating in each planetary body appears to us as heat in 3D, emerging from the most stable of all three-dimensional forms, the star tetrahedron.

The accurate mapping of the belt stars of Orion on the Earth in the three pyramids of Giza and the three henges of Thornborough show that the ancients sought to create a resonance with the stars of the Duat on the Earth.

The Pyramid texts state "Whoever shall make a copy of the Duat, and shall know it upon Earth, it shall act as a magical protector for him both in heaven and in Earth, unfailingly, regularly, and eternally."

This reminds me of science fiction writer Arthur C. Clarke's "three laws", especially his third law:

1. When a distinguished but elderly scientist states that something is possible, he is almost certainly right. When he states that something is impossible, he is very probably wrong.

2. The only way of discovering the limits of the possible is to venture a little way past them into the impossible.

3. Any sufficiently advanced technology is indistinguishable from magic.

I see our human bodies as magical containers for spirit. They allow our non-physical spirits to animate the flesh that can interact in this world. What spirit needs is a container, and better yet a vehicle for its embodiment in the physical realm. This container might be a human body, a suitably designed temple or architectural complex or city, a planet (the so called Gaia hypothesis) or perhaps as Rupert Sheldrake hypothesizes, the Sun.

Northumberlandia is the name of the "Lady of the North", a huge land sculpture in the shape of a reclining female figure some 1300 feet long. It is thought to be the largest land sculpture of the human form in the world and was officially opened by Princess Anne on August 29th, 2012. Perhaps it will resonate with a spirit? The fact that it is located at 55 degrees 5 minutes North to me suggests Isis might be the most likely candidate.

There is no known way to scientifically verify the embodiment of the goddess of nature in Northumberlandia because spirit is not physical, just as there is no way to prove to the satisfaction of materialists that you have any spirit whatsoever. Are you solely a biological machine or is there more to reality?

Any path to knowledge is a path to God—or Reality, whichever word one prefers to use. -Arthur C. Clarke

The many alignments that I have presented in this book suggest a human made or human modified hyper-dimensional resonant pattern arranged in a kind of planetary-scale grid. The topology of this grid is still emerging as more research is done by myself and many others.

The way that key numbers and patterns are encoded into cities and architecture is not random. The encoding bears the unmistakable signature of consciousness. Therefore the burning question is, "Who is the *encoder* behind the curtain?"

Encoders of the First Kind

Encoders of the first kind are humans involved in conspiracy. Architects are the most obvious encoders of sacred or secret knowledge in buildings. Considering that numerous buildings constructed over thousands of years are encoded in all the ways discussed in Chapter 7 - Taxonomy of Encoded Structures, this implies an multi-generational conspiracy of master builders. The word *conspiracy* comes from the Latin *con* "together" + *spirare* "breathe," meaning conspirators are people that breathe together to make a secret plan.

Many people suspect that the Freemasons, the Rosicrucians, or perhaps the Illuminati are ultimately behind this conspiracy. For example, the 33rd degree is the highest degree in the Scottish Rite. The George Washington National Masonic Memorial in Alexandria Virginia is 333 feet high. The distance from Nelson's column in Trafalgar Square (symbolically the center of England) to the center of 2012 London Olympic Stadium is 33,333 inches. The City of London is the 33rd jurisdiction surrounded by the 32 boroughs of greater London. You've seen many such examples with 33 and many other numbers throughout this book, and especially in Chapter 5 - Key Numbers and Chapter 8 - Encoded Structures. Did one of these groups plan all these things?

The Freemasons are a *society with secrets* but their existence is very well known in practically every city and town in the Western world. I myself am not a member of any society, secret or otherwise, and I don't have any special information on what goes on inside. However I have been contacted by and have had discussions with a few high ranking Scottish Rite Freemasons and Rosicrucians and in my limited experience they seem to me to be good, moral people who are genuinely interested in piecing together the puzzle of the universe just as much as I am. In my opinion, if there is a grand conspiracy within the many societies with secrets it would most likely come from the highest, most secretive levels within them or from some offshoot hidden organizations that exist in the shadows. Therefore any conspiracy within "societies with secrets" does not represent the vast majority of their membership.

The Illuminati on the other hand are supposedly a *secret society*. The official story is that Adam Weishaupt founded the Bavarian Illuminati on May 1, 1776 and it supposedly died out not long after. Conspiracy theorists argue convincingly that the Illuminati continue to this day amongst members of the global elite. However, no one outside the Illuminati definitively knows where their meetings or rituals are held or precisely who ranks among its members.

I just did a Google search on the word *Illuminati* and it returned an estimate of exactly 46,800,000 results (on 9/12/12). That is 864 backwards, a nice synchronicity between illumination and the number of the Sun! Obviously interest in this secret society is at an all time high or Google is part of the Illuminati conspiracy. I wouldn't rule that out for a company whose unofficial slogan is "Don't be evil"—guess what is hiding in their shadow?

We have heard about the Bohemian Grove, the Bilderberg Club, the Council of Foreign Relations, the Council for National Policy, and many other elite groups that meet in secret and decide how to rule the world, but what about groups that keep their existence truly secret?

Encodings are not just done in buildings; there are secrets in plain sight all around you. Many researchers have profiled Illuminati symbolism in corporate logos, movies, music, and pop culture. It is in your face these days and once you educate yourself about the symbols and rituals used, it is hard to miss Illuminati symbolism in events like Madonna's performance at the 2012 Superbowl halftime show or the opening and closing ceremonies of the 2012 London Olympics.

At the same time, the light of truth appears to be dawning in a big way and Bill Still, David Icke, Jim Mars, and hundreds of others have exposed numerous conspiracies. To deny the reality of conspiracy is becoming increasingly untenable for thinking people.

Amidst this global malaise I wonder if we don't give the Illuminati or whoever the human conspirators are far too much credit. Did the Illuminati or their progenitors construct the Dome of the Rock 33 miles from the sea and at the same time locate it 33.33 degrees from Stonehenge? Did they encode the meter so that the Earth's polar circumference would be 6/5 x 33,333,333 meters (99.98%)? Did they engineer the human spinal column to have 33 bones? Did they make the Sun 333,000 times more massive than the Earth?

Of course not!

The number 33 is a key embedded within the structure of reality. Recognizing that alone gives insight into one of the surprising ways in which the universe works. Over the centuries there have always been some who have recognized key numbers and symbols and encoded them in art, temples, cities, belief systems, and many other physical and conceptual structures. The practice of building in the microcosm to purposefully resonate with structures of the macrocosm is an ancient art of sympathetic magic. This art has continued to be practiced into modern times, for intentions that are not entirely clear.

Encoders of the Second Kind

Encoders of the second kind are physical extra-terrestrial beings. With billions of galaxies each containing billions of stars and an uncountable number of planets it is the depth of ignorance to assume that life exists only on the Earth.

Every year astronomers are finding more extrasolar Earth-like planets in the "Goldilocks zone" where the climate is favorable for human life. On 2/2/11, the Kepler Space Observatory Mission team released a list of 1235 extrasolar planet candidates, including 54 in the Goldilocks zone. The number of candidates goes up every year as astronomers see farther into space and with greater clarity.

In Chapter 4 - The Honeycomb and the Apple, I mentioned that on 8/8/11 NASA-funded astronomers announced the discovery of nucleobases found in 12 separate meteorites in Antarctica and how the precursors of life are therefore likely to be seeded throughout space. If life is indeed ubiquitous, intelligent life will have evolved in many places and indeed some species might be far more technologically advanced than we are. It follows that some of them have discovered a method to travel faster than light speed or to travel inter-dimensionally.

There have been approximately 100,000,000 UFO sightings worldwide since 1946.

To put it another way, on any particular evening there are around 1,000 sightings of UFO's around the USA (close encounters of the first kind), including 100 close encounters with the objects (close encounters of the second kind), 80 encounters with humanoids (close encounters of the third kind), and 15 abductions. -Luke Ford (http://anse.rs/PHK2H1)

The Disclosure Project is working to "fully disclose the facts about UFOs, extraterrestrial intelligence, and classified advanced energy and propulsion systems. We have over 500 government, military, and intelligence community witnesses testifying to their direct, personal, first hand experience with UFOs, ETs, ET technology, and the cover-up that keeps this information secret." (www.disclosureproject.org)

The Disclosure Project reveals that the extraterrestrial reality is far more complicated than is generally recognized, with testimony from individuals in secret military programs disclosing human interaction with more than 50 different extraterrestrial species.

A common question people have when they consider unidentified flying objects seriously is, "What are the intentions of the beings onboard?" If I pointed at an identified flying object such as a 747 flying overhead and asked, "What are the intentions of the beings on board?" you would perceive the gross oversimplification that such a question entails. There are at least as many intentions as there are species, and even within any one species individuals typically have widely differing intentions depending on the situation. Some ETs probably would like to help us evolve while others perhaps want to farm us for our psychic energy or use us for other nefarious purposes.

If humans have been interacting with different ET species in recent times, just how long has this been going on? Isn't it possible that ETs have been interacting with humans for thousands of years? Have they in fact been here all along? Did they even genetically engineer us as Zecharia Sitchin's (and many other authors) books suggest?

Interaction with ETs might explain how humans in the Neolithic era ended up encoding the speed of light in the Great Pyramid, and how advanced mathematical and astronomical knowledge was encoded into Stonehenge. It is possible that this interaction continues to this day and that some of the elite are literally doing the bidding of specific ET species.

The architects of encoded monuments might have understood reality on a much deeper level than the humans who actually built such complexes. I think that once a species gains knowledge of how the universe truly works, the tendency is to memorialize this understanding in plain sight.

The secret protects itself by virtue of its implausibility. -Idries Shah

Perhaps that is why we see encodings of Pi, Phi, e, 528, the relationship of 6 to 5, key numbers, and number patterns, in cities, temples, and units of measure. Monuments may bear witness to such high levels of understanding but we cannot decode such wisdom until we have grown to a level where we can appreciate it.

In 2012 we are poised on the knife edge between fascist enslavement, endless war, and environmental destruction on one hand, and on the other political transformation, personal and environmental healing technologies, advanced energy generation and propulsion systems, intelligent inter-species communication, and liberation. Which type of reality will you co-create?

Encoders of the Third Kind

Encoders of the third kind are non-physical spirits and/or hyper-dimensional beings. These include but are by no means limited to God, Allah, Lucifer, Satan, Ahriman, Archons, Osiris, Isis, Set, Hathor, Brahma, Vishnu, Shiva, El, Inanna, Marduk, angels, demons, djinns, astral beings, and myriad others.

Imagine for a moment that the spirits are as real as you are but they are not physical. Just because you can't see, touch, or measure them doesn't mean they don't exist or that they cannot have a profound effect on the material world.

At this moment of time, man due his physical knowledge sees everything through the eye of physicality, which is the mirage that has blinded him from the truth of creation and the real essence of creation. 'O man of existence, close your eyes to your physicality, to see the reality of existence in all realms of the universe.' -M.T. Keshe

In Science Set Free (2012), Dr. Rupert Sheldrake, argues that "the materialist ideology is moribund; under its sway, increasingly expensive research is reaping diminishing returns while societies around the world are paying the price." Sheldrake examines scientific dogmas such as "all of reality is material or physical; the world is a machine, made up of inanimate matter; nature is purposeless; consciousness is nothing but the physical activity of the brain; free will is an illusion; God exists only as an idea in human minds." Sheldrake convincingly argues that each of these is a belief system that science would be far better off without.

If you can get your mind around the encoders of the third kind then you will see that it solves some of the problems of a global conspiracy lasting thousands of years - immortal spirits would be the masterminds behind any such conspiracy and could influence elite people from every generation to do their bidding and encode knowledge however they saw fit.

Individuals under the influence of spirits might not necessarily be conscious of the process. Instead of seeing an overpowering biblical-style vision or hearing voices in one's head, one might simply have a feeling that building an 864 foot high temple in a specific location would be a good idea.

From any perspective other than the non-dual "now" state of consciousness that Eckhart Tolle has popularized, everything is in duality. In other words, there are portions of good and evil in all things. Spirits have different interests and agendas. The astral world is a zoo, teaming with myriad voices clamoring for your attention. It can be visited in near death experiences, in lucid dreams, by repeating mantras, in meditation, by ingesting entheogenic substances, or by many other means.

The astral world is a plane of existence that the soul crosses before and after death, populated by non-physical beings. This plane of existence was postulated in classical, medieval, Eastern and Western esoteric philosophies and mystery religions, and was popularized more recently in Theosophy and Rosicrucianism.

Being influenced by an astral spirit can be a terrifying or wonderful experience depending on what one's consciousness attracts to it by the Law of Similarity.

When the disciple is ready, the master will appear. -Buddha

The encoders of the third kind can also be thought of as hyper-dimensional beings. We measure objects with length, width, and height in three spatial dimensions. Four-dimensional beings experience a fourth spatial dimension perpendicular to the other three that we have a lot of difficulty visualizing.

What is God? He is length, width, height, and depth. -St. Bernard de Clairvaux

Four centuries before Christ, Plato described hyper-dimensional reality in his allegory of the cave that goes something like the following. We are prisoners chained in a cave and sit facing a blank wall. There's a fire outside the cave and unseen people are passing in front of it. We see shadows on the cave wall and mistake this reduced-dimensional illusion for reality.

With our limited prisoner-perception we imperfectly perceive higher dimensions as time.

Time does not flow, any more than space flows. It is we who are flowing, wanderers in a four-dimensional universe. Time is just the same measurement of space as is length, breadth, and height. - *Professor N. A. Oumoff (1911)*

However, the laws of Newtonian, Einsteinian, and quantum physics work equally well without time. Physicist Carlo Rovelli says, "It may be that the best way to think about quantum reality is to give up the notion of time—that the fundamental description of the universe must be timeless."

David Wilcock presented an intriguing model of time-as-space in his book The Source Field Investigations (Dutton 2011). He profiled the research of Dr. Dewey Larson who proposed that time is three-dimensional:

Larson named his theory the Reciprocal System because he felt that space and time were in a perfect opposite relationship to each other...a reciprocal relationship. Though most people believe space and time couldn't be more different, Larson said that's only because we've been conditioned to think that way. Instead, Larson now invites us to envision a parallel reality, all around us, which is just like the space we now see—in almost every way. This parallel reality would have solid objects and livable areas just like our own—made from the same atoms and molecules we see around us. Our scientists would normally think these atoms exist only as waves in this stage of their existence. Remember—a wave over here is a solid particle over there.

Wilcock uses the term *space-time* to refer to our conventional notion of 3 dimensions of space and 1 of time, and *time-space* to refer to the parallel reality where there are 3 dimensions of time and 1 of space. Wilcock explains,

If you stay perfectly still when you go into this parallel reality, you won't travel in time. It's only when you start moving around that you either go into the future or the past. Let's be clear that even though you could walk around and explore things, no one here in our [space-time] reality would be able to see you. Larson said that from our normal perspective on Earth, you would be stuck in space. From a quantum physics perspective, you would appear to have turned into a wave. If anyone could see you at all, you might look like the typical description of a ghost. Even though you are free to move around in this parallel universe, and you certainly can, all you're actually doing is moving around in time...That means moving from one location to another in this parallel reality is actually time travel.

From the perspective of hyper-dimensional beings, it would be very simple to travel in time-space to ancient Gaul, for example, and *somehow* influence the people who chose the site of the Isis temple that would later become Notre Dame de Paris, and likewise travel in time-space to 14th century Scotland and influence the builders of Rosslyn Chapel so that it would be situated 864,000 meters from Notre Dame to encode the solar diameter of 864,000 miles (99.9%). The hyper-dimensional beings would doubtless already know about the metric system which was invented or even seeded by them into the 18th century and have traveled in time-space to make the distance between Notre Dame and Rosslyn chapel fit this measurement. From our perspective this reasoning seems convoluted but it is straightforward in time-space where time is as plain to see as a landscape.

The mechanism of how this might be done is less clear, although presumably these hyper-dimensional beings might have the technology to transfer themselves bodily from time-space to space-time (and vice-versa) or perhaps from their perspective they engage in some form of astral projection into our realm to influence humans in space-time.

This hyper-dimensional process might be related to a technique that was developed by the US military called *remote viewing*, where highly trained psi-soldiers travel non-physically through both space and time and accurately describe remote targets in the past, present, and possible futures. To the best of my knowledge remote viewers do not influence people in different times but one wonders if this might indeed be possible.

Once you start seeing how illusory time is, you might start wondering about synchronicity. In my research I experience synchronicity frequently. People regularly email, instant message, post on my blog or Facebook wall, or Skype me often just the right piece of information without having any conventional means of knowing what I am actively looking for. At times I have the sense of being inexplicably guided by this phenomenon.

In addition, the time-prompt phenomenon seems to be related. I tend to look at the clock when it is a repetitive or sequential code such as 11:11, 12:34, 3:33, 5:55, and so on far more than common sense would suggest would be statistically reasonable. Is my subconscious prompting me to look at the clock at these moments or is this synchronicity reassuring me that I am on the right track when I do notice these moments in time? I wrote the following in my chapter of The Sync Book 2 (edited by Alan Green 2012):

My friend Andrew Barron instant messaged me requesting that I call him while he was having his car serviced and so I did. We were talking about how 33 comes up in his life in many unexpected ways. For example, right in front of him there was a little marble Honda award obelisk at the car dealership on top of a TV that was tuned to channel 33. Just then the service technician interrupted our conversation and I overheard him telling Andrew that his battery was tested as having 333 cold cranking amps.

The non-random nature of synchronicity suggests some kind of consciousness is behind it. But just who is behind it and why is much harder to ascertain. Why are the encoders of the third kind encoding sacred knowledge all around us? Perhaps they are doing it to teach us in a non-invasive way. Perhaps they know that we will learn and awaken to the deeper reality only when we are ready.

Encoders of the Fourth Kind

We ourselves are the encoders of the fourth kind. Colin Andrews told a pertinent story in his recent interview on Red Ice radio (http://bit.ly/Q0uiNG). I will paraphrase his story as follows.

A dozen women had a plan to meditate as a group in Wiltshire England and so they drove together without any preconceived destination. They ended up parking on the side of a country lane called 'the Avenue' close to Avebury. The women wandered into the adjacent field, spread out a few blankets under a copse of trees about 300 yards from the road and began meditating. During their meditation each one of the women independently arrived (without prior planning) with the same specific crop circle in their minds' eyes, which happened to be a small portion of the flower of life design. They also each projected in their minds that they would like this to appear close to them. When the women discussed this amongst themselves after the meditation they must have been amazed.

That same evening Matthew Williams, a crop circle maker (also known as a "hoaxer"), was watching television alone at home and as he described it, had a sudden out-of-nowhere urge to make a specific pattern that he saw in his head. He sat down and figured out how he would make it, got in his car and found himself parking along 'the Avenue.' He noticed a strange rapid temperature drop, but proceeded to make the crop circle with boards and strings. He heard voices less than 100 yards away in the trees and left the field after he finished his work. He made it his business in the coming days to find out who the voices belonged to. With the help of the local farmer and a number of people who had gardens that backed onto this area he discovered the voices belonged to the women meditators and eventually tracked down the leader of the group.

She informed him that yes it was her group and how they had each seen the same design in meditation and the very design arrived in that field that same night! Matthew Williams said, "Yes, and I made it."

But where did the design come from? Was it from the minds of the meditators, the mind of the maker, or from another source? I see this story as an allegory of what might be happening in other domains such as in architecture and urban design.

Wendy Flentri writes in her article "Crop Circle Phenomena and 2012" (http://bit.ly/SGUScE):

Matthew Williams justifies his group's [Circle Makers] activities by claiming it is good for local business by stimulating the tourist industry. He and his group feel compelled to go out late at night and spend five or so hours creating a crop circle with board, strings and roller. Why is he compelled; he has no answer for that. Researchers should bear in mind that they may be compelled by mind control agencies or extraterrestrials, especially since it seems the British Military are also creating circles according to Delgado and Andrews. This possibility is given further credence by Dr. Michael Salla, international political scholar who reports that the military are interested in crop circles and their extraterrestrial connection but downplay their official interest.

Colin Andrews estimated that humans make 80% of the crop circles. This estimate has angered many crop circle researchers who believe something like humans make only 20%. Whatever the percentage breakdown, we can probably all agree that crop circles are made by one or more of the kinds of encoders presented in this chapter.

All the world's a stage,
And all the men and women merely players;
They have their exits and their entrances,
And one man in his time plays many parts,
His acts being seven ages. -Shakespeare

Crop circles are a gentle means of geometric communication. The designs are available in the public domain for anyone with Internet access to study.

Do encoders leave keys to expanded awareness all around us in plain sight, hoping that we will someday take notice of them?

In a sense the Great Pyramid is a time capsule encoded to be decipherable once we have reached certain levels of understanding. This mute mountain of stone encrypts principles of sacred geometry, Pi, Phi, the speed of light, the size of the Earth, our systems of measurement, single repetitive digits, a shaft pointing to Sirius, and much more.

As scientists probed deeply into the microcosm in the 20th century they discovered that there is no real substance to the atom. If you were able to blow up an atom to the size of the London Olympic stadium, its nucleus would be approximately the size of a marble. Infinitesimal electrons blur in and out of existence according to the laws of probability in a cloud the size of the stadium. So what is in between the electrons and the nucleus? Nothing. Physical reality is 99.9999% empty space.

O Shariputra, form is no other than emptiness, emptiness no other than form. Form is exactly emptiness, emptiness exactly form. -The Great Prajna Paramita Heart Sutra of Buddhism

With the development of quantum mechanics, the common sense nature of reality was further called into question. Atoms themselves are continually phasing into and out of the vacuum of space-time in a process called quantum fluctuation...now they exist, now they don't.

Quantum tunneling is the process describing how a particle as large as a Buckyball (nano carbon soccer ball with atomic mass of

720) can be shot at a classically-impenetrable barrier, turn into a wave passing through two adjacent slits and pass through the wall, and then turn back into a Buckyball on the other side (proven by Dr. Olaf Nairz in 1999).

Einstein called quantum entanglement "spooky action at a distance," a process when two or more atoms, electrons or even molecules interact physically and then when they are separated, their quantum mechanical state remains linked no matter how far away the atoms are located from each other. This concept is a scientific case study of the Law of Contact or Contagion in sympathetic magic.

As astronomers have looked outward with terrestrial and space telescopes they have been able to more and more accurately measure the vastness of the macrocosm. Why should the circumference of the Sun be so beautifully equal to the circumference of the Earth times the circumference of the Moon divided by 100 (99.8%)? Why, as Lawrence Edlund discovered, should 1 inch / 1 mile = 1 astronomical unit / 1 light-year (99.9%)?

Scientists are slowly waking up to an inconvenient truth - the universe looks suspiciously like a fix. The issue concerns the very laws of nature themselves. For 40 years, physicists and cosmologists have been quietly collecting examples of all too convenient 'coincidences' and special features in the underlying laws of the universe that seem to be necessary in order for life, and hence conscious beings, to exist. Change any one of them and the consequences would be lethal. Fred Hoyle, the distinguished cosmologist, once said it was as if, 'a super-intellect has monkeyed with physics.' -Paul Davies, physicist

Reality is a riddle, wrapped in a mystery, folded inside an enigma; but perhaps there is a key.

As long as you still experience the stars as something 'above your head' you lack the eye of knowledge. -Friedrich Nietzsche

Everything above your head is also mirrored like a hologram inside your head. All is ultimately consciousness. If consciousness can arrange the macrocosm with such geometric and numerical perfection then perhaps we should not be that surprised that the things humans build in our particular microcosm often contain within them the keys for expanding our awareness.

Most of the facts in this book take a third-person approach. In other words, facts were presented about the world out there, no matter whether we are talking about planets, cities, architecture, or atoms.

This chapter has been about who the encoders might possibly be. That implies a second person relationship between us and them. Who are *they*, and why are *they* doing what *they* are doing? This leads to rounds of endless speculation and people will likely have different opinions about which kind of encoder is the most likely based on their current world view and personal experiences.

My personal opinion is that the encoders are simultaneously of all four kinds. Reality is amazingly diverse and complex. I feel that the ultimate truth of why secrets are encoded in plain sight is to be found within each of us. This is a first person perspective to the divinity of the universe, both outside and inside.

"I am that" and so are you.

About the Author

Scott Onstott is a teacher, writer, filmmaker, and artist. He has a degree in architecture from the University of California at Berkeley, has written or co-written 9 technical books on architectural design and visualization software, offers training videos on AutoCAD, Photoshop, 3ds max, and SketchUp, and creates digital art based on number and sacred geometry.

Scott Onstott has created a documentary series called Secrets In Plain Sight that explores patterns in art, architecture, urban design, and the cosmos.

Discover his other work at

http://www.secretsinplainsight.com and
http://www.scottonstott.com

40118914R00099

Made in the USA
Charleston, SC
24 March 2015